I like the book for today.

Earth in Action

Earthquakes

by Mari Schuh

Consulting Editor: Gail Saunders-Smith, PhD

Consultant: Susan L. Cutter, PhD
Carolina Distinguished Professor and Director,
Hazards & Vulnerability Research Institute
Department of Geography, University of South Carolina

Capstone press®

Mankato, Minnesota

Pebble Plus is published by Capstone Press,
1710 Roe Crest Drive, North Mankato, Minnesota 56003.
www.capstonepub.com

Library of Congress Cataloging-in-Publication Data
Schuh, Mari, 1975–
    Earthquakes / by Mari Schuh.
    p. cm. — (Pebble Plus. Earth in action)
    Summary: "Describes earthquakes, how they occur, and the damage they cause" — Provided by publisher.
    Includes bibliographical references and index.
    ISBN 978-1-4296-3436-6 (lib. bdg.)
    1. Earthquakes — Juvenile literature. I. Title. II. Series.
QE521.3.S378 2010
551.22 — dc22
                                    2009002169

Editorial Credits
Erika L. Shores, editor; Lori Bye, designer; Wanda Winch, media researcher

Photo Credits
Alamy/Roy Garner, 5
AP Images/Nick Ut, 21
Compass Point Books/Eric Hoffmann, 7
FEMA News Photo/Robert A. Eplett, 1
Getty Images Inc./AFP/Jes Aznar, 17; AFP/Liu Jin, 13; AFP/Teh Eng Koon, cover; David McNew, 15
Newscom/Kyodo, 19
Peter Arnold/Kevin Schafer, 11
Shutterstock/anthro, 9

The author dedicates this book to Margaret Wieboldt of Winthrop Harbor, Illinois.

Note to Parents and Teachers

The Earth in Action set supports national science standards related to earth science. This
book describes and illustrates earthquakes. The images support early readers in understanding
the text. The repetition of words and phrases helps early readers learn new words. This book
also introduces early readers to subject-specific vocabulary words, which are defined in the
Glossary section. Early readers may need assistance to read some words and to use the Table of
Contents, Glossary, Read More, Internet Sites, and Index sections of the book.

Printed in the United States of America in Stevens Point, Wisconsin.
072013
007607R

Table of Contents

What Is an Earthquake?

Earthquakes are the sudden

movement of the earth's surface.

Roads can bend and crack.

Buildings can fall.

How Earthquakes Happen

Earth's surface is called

the crust.

Huge pieces of rock

make up the crust.

These rocks are called plates.

Earth's Plates

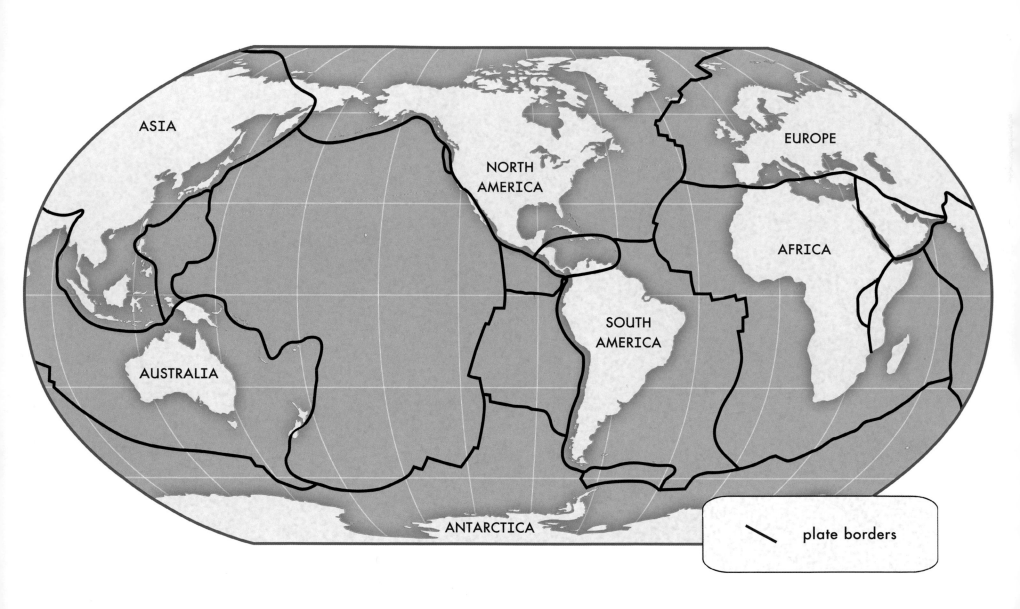

ASIA

EUROPE

NORTH
AMERICA

AFRICA

SOUTH
AMERICA

AUSTRALIA

ANTARCTICA

plate borders

Plates can push against each other. One plate can also move under another. Sudden movement shakes the earth.

How Plates Move

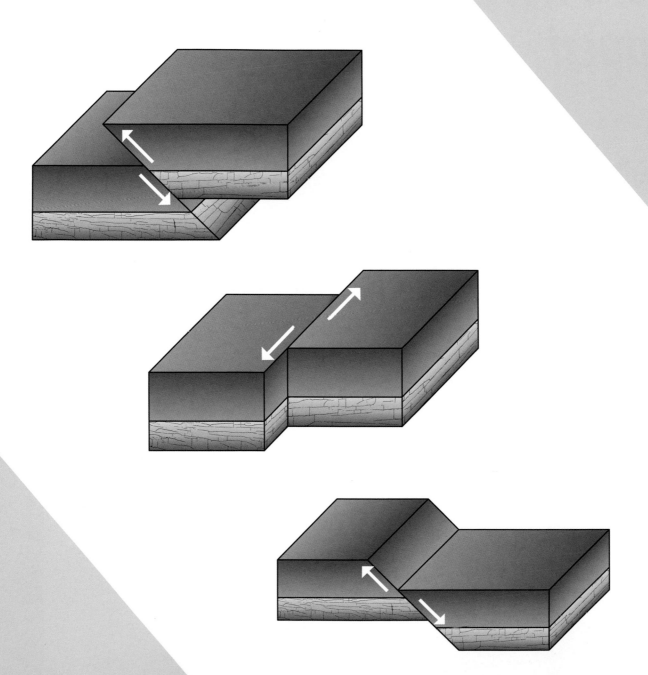

Where Earthquakes Happen

A fault is where the plates meet and rub together. Most earthquakes happen near faults.

fault

Staying Safe

Earthquakes happen

without warning.

If you are outside, get away

from buildings and trees.

Drop to the ground.

If you are inside,

move away from windows.

Drop to the floor and

hide under a desk or table.

Learning about Earthquakes

Scientists use seismographs

to measure earthquakes.

These machines record

how much the earth moves.

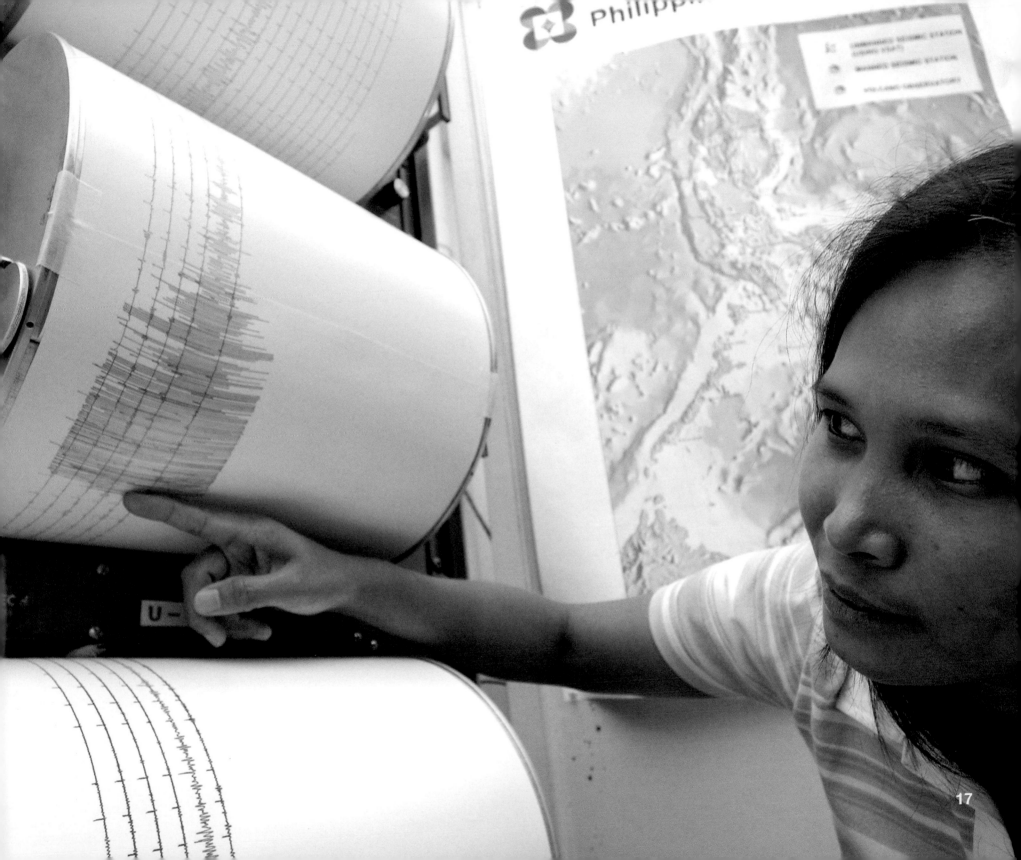

U-

Scientists use the Richter scale
to compare earthquakes.
Strong earthquakes measure
6.0 or higher on the scale.

Builders are making

stronger buildings

and bridges.

People work to keep us

safer when the ground shakes.

Glossary

crust — the hard outer layer of the earth

fault — a crack in earth's crust; some faults are just a few inches long; other faults stretch for hundreds of miles.

measure — to find out the size or strength of something

plate — a large sheet of rock that is a piece of earth's crust

Richter scale — a scale that measures the amount of energy in an earthquake; earthquakes with low numbers cause little or no damage.

scientist — a person who studies the world around us

seismograph — a machine used to measure earthquakes

Read More

Armentrout, David, and Patricia Armentrout. *Earthquakes.* Earth's Power. Vero Beach, Fla.: Rourke, 2007.

Harris, Nicholas. *Earthquakes through Time.* Fast Forward. New York: PowerKids Press, 2009.

Riley, Joelle. *Earthquakes.* Pull Ahead Books: Forces of Nature. Minneapolis: Lerner, 2008.

Internet Sites

FactHound offers a safe, fun way to find Internet sites related to this book. All of the sites on FactHound have been researched by our staff.

Here's all you do:
Visit *www.facthound.com*

FactHound will fetch the best sites for you!

Index

Word Count: 154

Grade: 1

Early-Intervention Level: 24

Patrisse Cullors Victoria B
e Sister Army Elizabeth D
nka Kosor Tyra Banks Rac
l Lee Brown Dr. Jasmin M
e Rosemarie Aquilina Sim
llen Bishop Vashti Murphy
Emme Amy Gutmann Be
sz The U.S. Women's Nation
hard Sherrilyn Ifill Shond
ardóttir Lupita Nyong'o C
se Kamla Persad-Bissessa
r Maya Rudolph Veronica
Giffords Samantha Fuent
e Joyner-Kersee Evelyn La
Nicole Kidman Julia Gilla
na Kiviniemi Tory Burch

30 YEARS OF
WOMEN
WHO HAVE RESHAPED THE WORLD

30 YEARS OF
WOMEN

WHO HAVE
RESHAPED THE
WORLD

Foreword by Yara Shahidi
Introduction by Samantha Barry, Editor in Chief
Text by Anna Moeslein
Edited by Natasha Pearlman

Abrams, New York

Text: Anna Moeslein
Design: Sarah Olin
Glamour Editor: Natasha Pearlman
Abrams Editor: Rebecca Kaplan
Abrams Production Manager: Anet Sirna-Bruder

Library of Congress Control Number: 2020943990

ISBN: 978-1-4197-5208-7
eISBN: 978-1-64700-289-3

Printed and bound in the United States
10 9 8 7 6 5 4 3 2 1

Abrams books are available at special discounts when purchased in quantity for premiums and promotions as well as fundraising or educational use. Special editions can also be created to specification. For details, contact specialsales@abramsbooks.com or the address below.

Abrams® is a registered trademark of Harry N. Abrams, Inc.

ABRAMS The Art of Books
195 Broadway, New York, NY 10007
abramsbooks.com

To all the Women of the Year—past, present, and those still to come.

TABLE
OF
CONTENTS

———

1
CHANGE MAKERS &
RULE BREAKERS

2
LEADERS & PIONEERS

3
VOICES & VISIONARIES

FOREWORD

———

I have not lived my young life believing that accolades would shape my path,

but the *Glamour* Woman of the Year (WOTY) Award is more than an accolade. WOTY celebrates women who place civic engagement squarely in front of their forward-facing talents and perceived fame. It brings together women who are actively doing work that is making a difference in the world—is that not the best one can aspire to? WOTY celebrates women who make an impact, which is a powerful testimony and statement in a world where their achievements have many times been overlooked.

Quite honestly, it was surreal to have been recognized as a 2019 *Glamour* Woman of the Year. My sincere admiration of the women honored before me only heightened my gratitude and deepened my commitment to our global community. It was rewarding to know that the work I continue to do in the spaces of voter education and civic engagement resonates with so many, and I am excited to be included in this extraordinary community.

Community is a word I keep coming back to when I speak of the Women of the Year Awards. The day I was to receive my honor in New York, I also had an obligation to be present in my Old English language class at Harvard University. So at 4 a.m. the morning of the awards, my father and I flew to Boston, where I attended class before returning to New York that same day for the awards ceremony. Even though I had been up since before sunrise, I was *so* excited about the upcoming evening that sleep was the furthest thing from my mind. To have the opportunity to connect with my fellow honorees—Ava DuVernay, Megan Rapinoe, the women of RAICES, Margaret Atwood, and others—felt like winning the lottery. I sat near Tory Burch, who started the Tory Burch Foundation to empower other women, and who once asked, at the foundation's 2018 Embrace Ambition Summit, a 16-year-old Yara what her dreams looked like (and then supported those dreams!). Every acceptance speech I heard that evening was a profound verbal rededication to the work each awardee was championing. Each sentence landed in my spirit as a confirmation of my own commitment to a purpose-driven life. I was overwhelmed by the genuine fellowship palpable in the room that evening.

It reminded me that we can rely on our support networks, or what my mother and grandfather lovingly speak of as "relationship equity." The voluntary pouring of personal energy into others, without expectation of reciprocation, organically builds a bevy of support around you. To know that we can rely on these relationships when in need is deeply moving. WOTY has created space for a community of women who actively build one another up and push forward, together, for equity in all spaces.

In 2020 so much of my work was centered around voter education. And because of our unusual predicament—coping with the COVID-19 pandemic while simultaneously being in another historic fight for the literal livelihood and civil rights of Brown and Black communities, while also needing every voice heard in the presidential election—WOTY's significance became even more important. I have thought back to that night, many a time, to uncover more inspiration and ways to be of service to my peers, who have made incredible strides for equity in communities significantly affected by violence, bias, and intimidation. And what is most inspiring is knowing that my peers are also leaders, community organizers, and artists orienting their skills and passions toward social justice.

In November 2020 I had the good fortune of being in conversation with the women known in politics as the Squad—congresswomen Alexandria Ocasio-Cortez, Ilhan Omar, Ayanna Pressley, and Rashida Tlaib, all of whom are united in their advocacy toward inclusive, progressive policies. I walked away with a deeper understanding that the 2020 presidential election was *not* about finding all the answers or solutions to our current and obvious discord. It was about setting the conditions, for us as women, to continue activating and pushing forward. It has been crystal clear that when we are in the middle of a literal battle to maintain and protect civil liberties, there is little space to see what the next steps *could* look like. But now, as more women like the Squad become decision makers, reimagining our future seems possible.

WOTY encourages us to think audaciously. It also shows us there are many ways to create spaces focused on supporting and uplifting one another, which has been reflected to me by my own family as well. I've always felt grateful to be supported by a family that believes it is our duty to be socially engaged, and to know that any opportunity one can provide to another person—a conversation, a connection, a supportive moment—is important and vital.

We are *all* capable of being active collaborators in someone else's journey, regardless of our work titles. We must remember that we are all in a position to help. We must remain open to the conversations and collaborations that will help others succeed. And we must remain committed to our global community, for it is the responsibility of each and every one of us to continue learning about the world and the richness of the vast number of people who make our world so beautiful. And, most important, we must be willing to bring others into spaces that may have been previously inaccessible. Let us continue to prepare the ground for one another and for the generations of incredible women who will surely follow.

—**YARA SHAHIDI**
actor, change agent, and
2019 Glamour *Woman of the Year*

At the very first Women of the Year Awards, in 1990,

Glamour's legendary editor in chief, Ruth Whitney, took to the stage at the Rainbow Room in New York and saluted the women "who have lit up 1990." The "doers," as she called them, the "darers," and the "defiers." Women who, as that year's special Women of the Year print issue also declared, "took charge, spoke out, risked their lives, made a difference."

Those very sentiments have formed the beating heart of *Glamour*'s annual celebration ever since. The women who defined the past three decades truly did take charge, speak out, defy, dare, and in some cases risk their lives to make a difference and play their part reshaping the world in which we live.

But Women of the Year is so much more than just one spectacular night each year. The awards have become a living, breathing history mapping out the evolution of women's power across the worlds of film, politics, sports, science, music, activism, literature, and more. They are also a symbol of a lifetime of achievement for some of the most extraordinary women around the globe. Which is why, as we approached our 30th anniversary, I wanted to take this moment in our heavily digital, often fleeting world to create a permanent testament to our honorees.

The achievements of our Women of the Year are phenomenal, and we hope that comes across in their deeply inspiring profiles. But it is *how* we celebrate them that is also important. We wanted to give great weight to their portraits. Imagery is so evocative, and it has always been vital for *Glamour* to capture our Women of the Year in a way that shows their power. I hope you experience that in your journey through this book.

It is also about service—the service of the women, and our service to you. I want you to read this book and leave with aspirations. I want to bring to life those spine-tingling acceptance speeches from the awards themselves that moved one thousand audience members to tears or standing ovations. I want you to read new interviews with our honorees and feel the sea of supporters behind *you* as you take on the next stage of your own life. I want to show you that in every industry, in every walk of life, in every country in the world, there are women out there beating their own drum, making their own rooms, and leaning into the word *ambition*. And for everybody who picks up this book, I want you not only to be inspired but to see yourself as the leading woman of the year in your own life.

As *Glamour*'s editor in chief since January 2018, I am truly privileged to continue the legacy that Whitney began.

Even before I started in my role, I understood the immensity and importance of *Glamour*'s Women of the Year Awards. There are many events and opportunities to celebrate women today, but 30 years ago *Glamour* was among the first. As a result, we hold in the *Glamour* archives a wonderful history of the evolution of women's power and achievement. It is my job, as the steward of *Glamour*, to ensure that this rich legacy lives on and continues to advance.

My first Women of the Year Awards as editor in chief, in November 2018, will never leave me. It was an honor to help bring together so many spectacular women—we awarded Viola Davis, Manal al-Sharif, Betty Reid Soskin, Chrissy Teigen, Kamala Harris, Janelle Monáe, Judge Rosemarie Aquilina, the women activists from the Never Again movement, and the Sister Army of survivors who had brought the man who had sexually abused them to justice.

We had also arranged for Hillary Clinton to come to the awards, as a surprise, to honor all the women who had done so well in the midterm elections. Only I and a handful of others knew about her appearance. So after Monáe and Harris had accepted their awards, I got pulled out of my seat to greet Clinton backstage. We were there, waiting to go and surprise the audience, when al-Sharif—the Saudi activist who risked her life to protest for the right of women to drive in Saudi Arabia—finished her speech and walked offstage. She saw Clinton for the first time and reacted with the same kind of shock that everybody else in the audience was about to feel.

Clinton, who was secretary of state when al-Sharif was in prison and spoke out in support of her at the time, walked straight up to her and took al-Sharif's hand in hers. It was an electric, intimate moment in this tiny enclosed space—one that demonstrated to me the true beauty of Women of the Year and its ability not just to spotlight incredible women but also to bring them together for a night of celebration and to create connections.

That's at the heart of what Whitney set out to do three decades ago—to grow a *lifetime* network of women supporting women (which you can read more about on page 230).

I am forever blown away by our honorees' achievements in the years that we recognized them—and also their legacies beyond. Many of *Glamour*'s Women of the Year have experienced their greatest moments in the years after they were awarded. *Glamour*'s own legacy is that we honored them for that very reason—because we *knew* they were already women of greatness, with so much yet to give.

And that is why this book is so important. *Glamour*'s Women of the Year should rightly take their place not just in the archives of the magazine but also in the physical history books.

Every single year I learn something new about women's power. And this book is a testament to what we can all achieve when we work together. I want to thank our honorees for all that they have done and continue to do. I want to thank the teams at *Glamour*, who have worked tirelessly over 30 years to plan the magazine issues and events. And I want to thank the team that brought this book to life—a true labor of love. Women of the Year is a celebration of women. All women.

Each November, I sit in the Women of the Year audience not just as an editor in chief but as a woman with my own ambitions and my own desire to learn. I'm inspired when 2019 Woman of the Year Ava DuVernay says, "I don't want a chair at the table…I want the table to be rebuilt." I'm blown away when assault survivor and 2016 Woman of the Year Chanel Miller (read more about her story on page 260) stands up and owns her identity and story onstage, as she did three years later in 2019. It is truly the greatest honor of my life to be part of this legacy and to play a small role in shaping its future, not just for *Glamour* but for you.

I mean it when I say that every one of you could be a Woman of the Year. Yes, I want you to enjoy this book and the beautiful images contained within. But I also want you to be inspired. To finish the book believing in the power of your own ability. You are the woman of the year of your own life. *Glamour*'s honorees have reshaped the world we live in today, and so can you.

—**SAMANTHA BARRY**
editor in chief, 2018–present

1990

Since the very first Women of the Year Awards, in 1990, *Glamour* has honored women who achieve amazing successes–they take risks, speak up for what they believe in, fight for change, and carve new paths. And when you put these incredible visionaries in a room together, great things are bound to happen. Here we reflect on the past three decades with some of WOTY's best moments.

1990

The first Women of the Year Awards was held in NYC's Rainbow Room. Among the winners was Children's Defense Fund founder Marian Wright Edelman, who said, "If you don't like the way the world is, you change it."

1991

Anita Hill (1) was honored less than a month after she bravely testified in front of an all-male Senate Judiciary Committee about the sexual harassment she experienced from Supreme Court Justice Clarence Thomas.

1992

A record 24 women were elected to Congress in 1992, which became known as the "Year of the Woman." Carol Moseley Braun, the first Black woman to be elected to the U.S. Senate, was among those recognized at that year's ceremony.

1993

Fresh off the box office success of her movie *Sleepless in Seattle,* writer and director Nora Ephron picked up a WOTY Award. "This is the greatest job in the world," she said about her career.

1994
Winner Vanessa Williams rushed straight from the Women of the Year ceremony to the Broadway stage, where she had an 8:00 show that night as the lead in the Tony Award–winning *Kiss of the Spider Woman*.

1995
Madeleine Albright (2) was honored as the United States ambassador to the United Nations. "There are no bounds to what can happen when women get involved," she said in her speech. Less than two years later, she became the first woman secretary of state in U.S. history.

1996
U.S. Representative Susan Molinari, the top-ranking Republican woman at the time, was among that year's winners. She had made headlines for wearing pants on the House floor—unheard of at the time.

1997
Julia Louis-Dreyfus gave her acceptance speech in a prerecorded video from the *Seinfeld* set. "I didn't get into this business for the money, or the creative satisfaction, or the joy of performing," she quipped. "I got into it for something a little more meaningful: *the glamour*."

1998
The audience was moved to tears after hearing model **Waris Dirie's (3)** harrowing story about the genital mutilation she was subjected to at five years old and her fight to end the practice worldwide.

1999
TV's first woman network news coanchor, Barbara Walters, said it was surprising to receive that year's lifetime achievement award decades into her career because, at 61, "I'm still in there pitching and catching!"

2000
Vashti Murphy McKenzie (4), the first woman to become a bishop in the African Methodist Episcopal Church, gave one of the best quotes of the night: "Now since the stained-glass ceiling has been broken, don't you dare pick up the pieces and put it back."

2001
Two months after 9/11, *Glamour* honored rescue workers who lost their lives and RAWA, a group of women dedicated to fighting for social justice in Afghanistan. Says former *Glamour* editor in chief Cindi Leive, "It was important we recognized both the American heroes as well as the women who had been fighting and living under extremism for years."

2002
Angela Bassett presented **Nancy Pelosi (5),** then the House minority whip, with her first WOTY (the second came in 2007). "Every generation has a responsibility to make the future better for the next," the future Speaker of the House said.

2003
Seven months after their release from captivity in Iraq, honorees Private First Class Jessica Lynch and Specialist Shoshana Johnson paid tribute to Specialist Lori Ann Piestewa, the first servicewoman to be killed in the Iraq War and the first Native woman to die in combat while serving the U.S.

2004
"Damn, I'm too cool to cry!" **Alicia Keys (6)** said before citing her mother and grandmother as role models. "They taught me that you can still be beautiful even with all of our flaws."

2005

Woman of the Year Mukhtar Mai sought justice from her rapists—then used the money the Pakistani government gave her in compensation to start schools in her hometown. "It's because of the support of the world that I feel brave," she said.

2006
Future senator **Tammy Duckworth (7)** was running for Congress when she was honored as a Woman of the Year. "Stand up for what's important to you," she said. "Or someone else will make decisions for you."

2007
Mariah Carey (8), a 1998 Woman of the Year, opened the show with a moving performance of her hit song "Hero" alongside a children's choir. Toni Morrison, Shonda Rhimes, and Jennifer Garner were also celebrated for their achievements that year.

2008
Nujood Ali, the first child bride in Yemen to receive a divorce, and fellow honoree Hillary Clinton formed a bond when they met at the Women of the Year Awards. The two stayed in touch—when Clinton traveled to Yemen in 2011, Ali was one of the first people she met with—and the secretary of state joined the young activist in advocating to end the practice of child marriage worldwide.

2009
Lifetime achievement award winner Maya Angelou delivered one of the most memorable speeches in WOTY history. "Glamour is profound," she said. "It's saying, I take responsibility for myself."

2010

Glamour and the nonprofit Vital Voices created a fund for human rights activists **Dr. Hawa Abdi and her daughters (9),** who sheltered thousands of Somali refugees. Fellow honoree Julia Roberts was among those who pledged support.

2011
Jennifer Lopez (10), 1999 and 2011 Woman of the Year, championed the importance of sisterhood. "Support other women. Your girls are the most loyal people in your life. They will always be there. Those are my greatest loves."

2012
Ruth Bader Ginsburg (11), also a 1993 Woman of the Year, received her second WOTY. "Most of my life my lucky number has been two," she remarked, citing her milestones as the second woman to be appointed to the U.S. Court of Appeals as well as the Supreme Court.

2020

2015

Comedian Amy Schumer hosted the evening at New York City's Carnegie Hall and had the audience roaring with her opening remarks. One hilarious example: "I met [1995 winner] Madeleine Albright tonight and we *really* hit it off, so, you've got squad competition."

2016

"Black Lives Matter is more needed today than ever before," Black Lives Matter cofounder **Alicia Garza** said as she accepted the award alongside **Patrisse Cullors** and **Opal Tometi (12)** just six days after the 2016 presidential election. "This is not the time for us to sit back and wonder what we're going to do."

2014

"That I am included in this amazing group of women is... appropriate," Mindy Kaling said as she accepted her award. "I'm kind of a big deal." She may have been joking, but we agree: She *is* a big deal.

2013

Congresswoman turned gun-control advocate Gabby Giffords joined her husband, Mark Kelly, on stage two years after a gunman nearly took her life. "I'm still fighting to make the world a better place," she said.

2017

"You recognize when a leader is dangerous, even if that leader is the president of the United States of America," Congresswoman Maxine Waters said on stage at Kings Theatre in Brooklyn. In her speech, she addressed the young women in the audience, telling them, "You are smart, you are bright, you are intelligent, and I don't want you to be intimidated by anything or anybody."

2018

Two years before she became 2020 presidential candidate Joe Biden's running mate, Kamala Harris delivered a powerful message about leadership: "Years from now...people will ask, 'Where were you?' And we're all going to be able to say, 'Fighting for the best of who we are.'"

2019

When sexual assault survivor Chanel Miller was named a Woman of the Year in 2016, she chose to remain anonymous. Three years later she came forward and accepted her award on stage at Lincoln Center.

2020

The women nurses and doctors of Elmhurst Hospital, one of the many front lines in the battle against the coronavirus pandemic, were honored for their heroic work caring for critically ill COVID-19 patients.

CHANGE MAKERS & RULE BREAKERS

*Advocates, activists, champions,
and fighters—these women
speak up and demand progress
to make our world a better place.*

The Activists of Never Again

WOMEN OF THE YEAR 2018

On Valentine's Day 2018, a gunman with an AR-15 killed 17 students and staff at Marjory Stoneman Douglas High School in Parkland, Florida. Within hours politicians across the country were issuing statements of condolences—but a group of brave student survivors who wanted real change, not offers of "thoughts and prayers," had already formed.

Their targets: the president, the National Rifle Association—in fact, *all* those who supported lax gun policies. And the change: more stringent gun ownership laws, more accountability for the gun lobby and industry, and more people registered to vote to demand these actions.

Emma González, Jaclyn Corin, Samantha Fuentes, and their classmates reached out via social media to other student gun-control activists, including Edna Chavez and Naomi Wadler, to join them in creating March for Our Lives. Together the group registered thousands of votes, raised more than $100,000 for gun violence–prevention organizations, and led a march that saw more than 1 million people turn out in demonstrations across the country—one of the largest single days of protest against gun violence in U.S. history.

Their real goal, González told *Glamour* in 2018, was to solve the gun problem so March for Our Lives didn't have to exist. Ultimately, they wanted their story of loss and destruction to be the last. Sadly, there would be 337 mass shootings that year. "The world might be cruel," Fuentes said in the Women of the Year profile, "but you don't have to be. Though it might seem our leaders have forgotten the lives lost, and the TV screens are painted with terror, loss, and discouragement, you must not succumb to silence. To remain voiceless is to remain powerless."

These high school students proved that in a digital age, nobody has to remain voiceless. Through their activism, they took on the seemingly untouchable gun lobby and turned their movement into something much bigger. This is how you change the world.

Photographed in Washington, D.C., in 2018 are (top, from left): Samantha Fuentes, Emma González; (bottom, from left): Jaclyn Corin, Edna Chavez, and Naomi Wadler.

Lupita Nyong'o

WOMAN OF THE YEAR 2014

Before Lupita Nyong'o even graduated from Yale University, in 2012, she had scored her first feature role—in *12 Years a Slave*, a biographical film about Solomon Northup, a free Black man who was kidnapped and sold into slavery in the 1800s. Playing Patsey, a woman who befriends Northup on the plantation where he is taken, catapulted Nyong'o onto the world's stage. In the months following the film's release, she won the 2014 Oscar for Best Supporting Actress, was named the first Black spokeswoman of beauty brand Lancôme, and landed parts in two major Hollywood films. Later that year, in recognition of her extraordinary breakthrough, she was honored at *Glamour*'s Woman of the Year Awards.

Since then Nyong'o has continued to influence through her work onscreen. From bankable superhero films including *Black Panther* (2018) to culture-defining movies such as Jordan Peele's horror epic *Us* (2019), she has used her platform to showcase complex, uncompromising women. Away from the camera she has worked even harder to advocate for a variety of important causes and call out the colorism and racism issues that continue to plague Hollywood. In 2017 she wrote an essay for the *New York Times* in which she revealed that film producer Harvey Weinstein had sexually harassed her while she was a student at Yale. She committed to working only with directors who had not abused their power.

"I believe in listening to my gut and having a good relationship with my own instinct," she told *Glamour* in her 2014 interview, "because that will steer me where I need to go."

That instinct has propelled Nyong'o forward. Alongside her acting and advocacy, in 2019 she added children's author to her résumé with the publication of her debut book, *Sulwe*, a story of a young girl that encompasses colorism and the path to self-love and acceptance. "I've heard people talk about images in popular culture changing, and that makes me feel great because it means that the little girl I was, once upon a time, has an image to instill in her that she is beautiful, that she is worthy—that she can," she said. "Until I saw people who looked like me, doing the things I wanted to, I wasn't so sure it was a possibility. Seeing Whoopi Goldberg and Oprah in *The Color Purple,* it dawned on me: Oh—I could be an actress! We plant the seed of possibility."

"Every time I overcome an obstacle," Lupita Nyong'o said, "it feels like success. Sometimes the biggest ones are in our head—the saboteurs that tell us we can't."

Nadia Murad,
in the rose garden
at the United
Nations in 2016.

Nadia Murad

WOMAN OF THE YEAR 2016

For Nadia Murad, a survivor of the Islamic State of Iraq and Syria (ISIS), justice doesn't mean more violence. The militant group held her captive for three excruciating months in 2014, and she experienced firsthand the atrocities that ISIS was capable of. But instead of straightforward revenge, "I want them to hear the five-year-old boy they kidnapped and the nine-year-old girl they raped and the 30-year-old mother whose children they killed," she told *Glamour* in 2016 when she accepted her Woman of the Year Award. "By listening to their victims, I want them to *feel* what they've done."

To accomplish that, Murad devoted her life to sharing not just her own terrible experiences of rape and torture but also the stories of many, many others. It became her mission to tell the world about the genocide and destruction of the Yazidi people, an ethno-religious minority group in northern Iraq. "I want people to know this isn't what happened only to Nadia," she said. "This happened to thousands of girls. I want the world to know."

Nadia was just 19 when she was taken captive, sold into slavery, and held prisoner in Mosul, northern Iraq. She escaped when, by chance, her captor left the house unlocked. With the help of a neighbor, she was smuggled into Kurdistan, followed by a refugee camp in the Kurdish region of Duhok, and then, eventually, a new home in Germany. Once safe outside of ISIS territory, she started sharing her testimony about the rape, beatings, and other torture she had survived. Her words were so powerful that Yazda, an organization founded to support Yazidis, brought her to the United States to address the United Nations. But ISIS took notice too and started issuing death threats and finding increasingly disturbing ways to harass her. Her own nephew called, demanding that she return to ISIS-held territory. Murad didn't back down. Instead, in 2018, she started a global initiative against genocide and partnered with other powerful activists and organizations around the world to bring ISIS to justice. In 2018 she was awarded a Nobel Peace Prize for her efforts.

"I'm not afraid of them," she told *Glamour*. "What more can they do to me? There's no place in me for fear now."

how to create change,

BY THE CHANGE MAKERS THEMSELVES

The women Glamour *has honored over the years have taken action even when all the odds seemed stacked against them—but they all had to start somewhere. Here* Glamour *Women of the Year Award winners share their advice for how to inspire change.*

FIND YOUR CREW.

"I'd say three things to *Glamour* readers. One, trust your own voice. Two, do what you love. And three, have a group, maybe 5 or 12 people, who share your values, who make you feel smart—and get together with them at least once a month."

—GLORIA STEINEM, FEMINIST, JOURNALIST, AUTHOR, AND ACTIVIST AND 2011 WOMAN OF THE YEAR

START. *NOW.*

"I'm like a lot of women: We think we have to be perfect in every way. And so it's hard for us to take chances and do things where we think we might not measure up. But I remembered the most important lesson my mother taught me. She said, 'This is the only life you have. You have one chance to make a difference in the world. There are no do-overs. So do it now.'"

—CECILE RICHARDS, FORMER PRESIDENT OF PLANNED PARENTHOOD AND 2015 WOMAN OF THE YEAR

OWN YOUR POWER.

"Women are strong. Women can do anything. Come out and struggle for your rights; nothing can happen without your voice. Do not wait for me to do something for your rights. It's your world, and you can change it."

—MALALA YOUSAFZAI, ACTIVIST AND 2013 WOMAN OF THE YEAR

TAKE ACTION.

"When you see something happening, you don't just stand there. Knowing something is wrong and not doing anything is basically like doing it. You have to learn to appreciate yourself and the power you hold. Whatever is inside of you—your soul, your power—find it. See it. Respect it. Protect it. And use it."

—ZENDAYA, ACTOR AND 2016 WOMAN OF THE YEAR

KEEP FIGHTING.

"There is so much at stake, you cannot just give up like that. You have to do everything you can, even if everything seems hopeless. You have to do it."

—GRETA THUNBERG, ENVIRONMENTALIST AND 2019 WOMAN OF THE YEAR

ALWAYS BE LEARNING.

"When I was younger, I realized that education is everything. It gives you choices."

—ORAL LEE BROWN, EDUCATION ACTIVIST AND 2002 WOMAN OF THE YEAR

TAKE IT ONE STEP AT A TIME.

"There's great reason for optimism. Most people would like to do something to make the world a better place. You can't solve all the problems of the world, but each day you can do *something.* A certain peace comes from doing what you feel you should be doing."

—JANE GOODALL, CONSERVATION ACTIVIST AND 2008 WOMAN OF THE YEAR

SPEAK OUT.

"You must not succumb to silence. To remain voiceless is to remain powerless."

—SAMANTHA FUENTES, GUN-CONTROL ACTIVIST AND 2018 WOMAN OF THE YEAR

Misty Copeland

WOMAN OF THE YEAR 2015

Misty Copeland was living in a motel with her mom and five siblings when her teacher suggested she try ballet at the local Boys & Girls Clubs of America. Copeland was 13—much older than when most professional ballerinas begin their training—but she was hooked.

After 20 years of hard work, adversity, and a near career-ending injury (in 2012 she fractured her foot so badly she was told she might never dance again), Copeland was named the principal dancer at the American Ballet Theatre in New York City on June 30, 2015, at the age of 33. This made her the first Black woman to reach that level in the elite company's 75-year history.

"I think it's important for women to see themselves represented in every hue, in every shape, with different careers and different paths," she said in her *Glamour* Woman of the Year interview. "So I feel like I represent a lot of people."

Because of Copeland, young girls of color now have a role model in a profession that traditionally did not value Black and Brown dancers. Copeland continued to advocate for greater representation, and through her ongoing work with the Boys & Girls Clubs of America, she has mentored young girls who dream that they too might become principal ballerinas one day. "My message to young women," she said, "would be to love yourself, to believe in yourself, and to not let other people's words get in the way and distract you or define you."

31

"Be st
be fe
be be

rong,
arless,
autiful."

The Guardians of Elmhurst

WOMEN OF THE YEAR 2020

In January 2020 the first case of COVID-19 in the U.S. was confirmed. Much was still unknown about the deadly virus, but reports from China and other parts of the world were already detailing the horrific effects of the disease.

Two months later, on March 11, the World Health Organization declared the virus a pandemic. On that day alone there were 7,136 new cases and 344 reported deaths around the world. People mourned the loss of their loved ones and started sheltering in place, unsure of when they'd be with friends and family again. Countries started closing their borders. Businesses shut their doors not knowing when—or if—they would reopen.

New York City rapidly became one of the first epicenters of cases in the country. (By September 2020 the virus had infected more than 237,000 people there.) At NYC Health + Hospitals/Elmhurst, a teaching medical center in Queens that serves one of the most diverse zip codes in the U.S., the staff was preparing for battle. In February the facility had been designated as one of a few receiving hospitals for all the city's coronavirus cases, making it one of the most crucial front lines against the virus in the country. More than 7,000 cases were reported in central Queens alone within the first weeks of the outbreak. The strain on Elmhurst's staff, and its entire infrastructure, was felt immediately. Queens had just 1.5 hospital beds per 1,000 people, compared with 5.3 in Manhattan, and Elmhurst was accepting 125 percent of its maximum intake.

Almost 4,000 people work at Elmhurst—and nearly 3,000 of them are women, all of whom have risked their lives to provide care. At *Glamour*'s 2020 WOTY Awards, we honored four of these women by name—but they stood for everyone at the hospital. Each represents the breadth of roles needed to keep a hospital running, as well as the immense contributions and sacrifices that women caretakers and essential workers around the world have made in the fight against this disease.

They are Navdeep Kaur, a critical care nurse in the ICU who contracted and survived coronavirus while providing care; Meida Sanchez, who would comfort the patients while working as a cleaner; Veronica Henry, the director of the department of pathology, who worked around the clock to deliver accurate and fast lab results; and Jasmin Moshirpur, M.D., the chief medical officer for NYC Health + Hospitals/Elmhurst/Queens and the dean for Elmhurst/Queens Programs at the Icahn School of Medicine at Mount Sinai, who, at 82, was at high risk of severe illness from the disease but still came to work every day to steer the hospital through an unprecedented chapter in history.

Moshirpur has been practicing for over five decades, but the pandemic was unlike anything she'd experienced. "What will stay with me for the rest of my life—and I don't know how many more years that I have—is the teamwork," she said.

"We tried to be good people, to be more close to each other, to try to work together," Sanchez said. "So many, many of us changed. We are different."

From left: Veronica Henry, director of the department of pathology; Navdeep Kaur, critical care nurse (ICU); Meida Sanchez, housekeeping department; and Jasmin Moshirpur, M.D., chief medical officer for NYC Health + Hospitals/Elmhurst/Queens are photographed outside Elmhurst Hospital.

Rihanna

WOMAN OF THE YEAR 2009

At 21, Rihanna was honored as a *Glamour* Woman of the Year after she had won over the rest of the country with her signature It factor. Her refusal to play by pop's cookie-cutter rules was, for a heavily controlled industry, revolutionary, and the number-one hits and millions of album sales soon followed.

But she was already more than a music superstar. When *Glamour* named her Woman of the Year in 2009, she had started the Believe Foundation, a fund to provide educational and medical assistance to children in need. She had also used her platform to speak out on behalf of domestic violence survivors after her own assault at the hands of a former boyfriend, that same year, had become public. "My story was broadcast all over the world for people to see, and they have followed every step of my recovery," she told *Glamour*. "The positive thing that has come out of my situation is that people can learn from that. I want to give as much insight as I can to young women because I feel like I represent a voice that really isn't heard. Now I can help speak for those women."

The year 2009 marked only the beginning of her trailblazing career and accomplishments. In 2012 she launched the Clara Lionel Foundation, an education and emergency response program, in honor of her grandparents. In 2017 she completely upended the fashion and beauty industries with the launch of her inclusive Fenty line. And in 2020, as COVID-19 swept the world, Rihanna's foundation donated $5 million for relief efforts in the U.S., the Caribbean, and Africa.

For Rihanna there is no ceiling to her ambitions. "What I want is to continue to grow," she told *Glamour*. "Because I am never satisfied; I always want more. I always want to get better. I always want to climb another step."

"I want to give as much insight as I can to young women," Rihanna told *Glamour* in 2009, "because I feel like I represent a voice that really isn't heard."

The Women Behind Black Lives Matter

History has shown that a global movement can begin anywhere—even, as in this instance, a Facebook post.

In 2013, George Zimmerman, the neighborhood watch volunteer who shot and killed 17-year-old Trayvon Martin, a Black high school student who had simply been walking down the street on his way to visit his dad's fiancée, was acquitted on all charges. Longtime activist Alicia Garza was devastated. It could have been her brother who was killed, she thought. It could have been any member of her family. Any Black person. Garza spent the evening texting with her friend, Los Angeles–based organizer and artist Patrisse Cullors. By the morning she was ready to take action. On her Facebook page she wrote, in a series of now famous posts, "I continue to be surprised at how little Black lives matter...Black people. I love you. I love us. Our lives matter."

Cullors shared the posts, adding the hashtag #BlackLivesMatter. When Opal Tometi, the executive director of the Black Alliance for Just Immigration, saw it, she reached out. "I felt a sense of urgency about the next steps we could take together to change the story," Tometi told *Glamour* in 2016.

And change the story they did: #BlackLivesMatter became a generation-defining global movement for fighting systemic racism, increasing anti-racism education, and fostering greater equality. By 2020 the hashtag had been used nearly 48 million times on Twitter. The Black Lives Matter Global Network, a decentralized coalition of 17 autonomous chapters in the United States and Canada, was created to do work in local communities. Children, adults, politicians, activists, celebrities, and diverse religious and cultural communities came together to demand meaningful change, police reform, and justice for the many Black lives lost at the hands of law enforcement and beyond. The work Garza, Cullors, and Tometi started in 2016 is far from finished, but it laid the foundation for a global phenomenon. In 2020, as millions around the world took to the streets to demand accountability in the wake of the deaths of George Floyd, Breonna Taylor, and so many more, their impact continued to be felt.

"We gave tongue to something that we all knew was happening," Tometi said. "We were courageous enough to call it what it was. But more than that, to offer an alternative. An aspirational message: Black lives matter."

The women behind Black Lives Matter, from left: Alicia Garza, Opal Tometi, and Patrisse Cullors.

Kamala Harris

WOMAN OF THE YEAR 2018

From her earliest days, Kamala Harris learned how to speak truth to power. Her parents—both immigrants to the United States—met as activists in the civil rights movement, and they'd bring a young Harris with them to marches. "It was the '60s and '70s, a charged time where everyone in my life was very actively involved," Harris told *Glamour* in her 2018 Woman of the Year profile. "One of the soundtracks of my childhood is 'Young, Gifted and Black.' It was about being told you can do anything you want to do."

What Harris wanted to do was create change from the inside, where the decisions were made. Elected in 2016, the senator—the lone Black woman in the chamber at the time and the first-ever South Asian American—used her experience as a prosecutor and an attorney general to fight for legislation around issues like bail reform and civil rights. Her blunt, pull-no-punches approach garnered her fans and enemies in equal numbers. During the 2018 Senate hearings for Supreme Court Justice Brett Kavanaugh, for example, Harris went viral for schooling the then nominee on reproductive rights so much that he stumbled over his own words. "One of the things that all leaders need to do is speak truth," she said at the time. "Even if it's an uncomfortable truth."

Harris's commitment to creating change led her to run for president in 2020. Though she eventually withdrew from the race, it was far from the last time Harris was central in American politics. In August that year, Democratic presidential candidate Joe Biden selected Harris to be his running mate. When the election was called that November, she became not only the first woman vice president-elect but the first Black and South Asian American woman to reach that executive level. "Years from now, people are going to look in our eyes," Harris said in her WOTY acceptance speech. "And they will ask us, 'Where were you?' And what we're all going to be able to say is we were fighting for the best of who we are."

"My mother always told me, 'You may be the first to do many things,'" said Kamala Harris in 2018. "'Make sure you're not the last.'"

"THE TRUTH—AND SPEAKING IT— IS A POWERFUL THING."

In November 2020, Kamala Harris made history. As president-elect Joe Biden's running mate, Harris became the first Black and South Asian American woman to be elected vice president. And though Harris is the third woman to become a vice presidential nominee, none has ever held the post in America's 244 years—until now. "While I may be the first woman in this office, I will not be the last," she said hours after the election was called. "Because every little girl watching tonight sees that this is a country of possibilities." And like all those heroic and ambitious women before her, Harris has inspired others to action through her leadership. That was especially on display in her stirring speech at the 2018 WOTY Awards, which you can read in full here.

THERE ARE PHENOMENAL WOMEN here who have been past recipients, who are present recipients, and who have been leaders in our country, and I couldn't be more honored to be a part of this evening. I will say, looking across the honorees tonight, there is one thing you all have in common with each other, and it is something this country needs more of, and that is to speak truth and have leaders who speak truth.

Here's the thing about truth. The truth—and speaking it—is a powerful thing. And speaking truth can often make people quite uncomfortable, but if we are going to be a country that engages in honest conversations with the point of getting beyond where we are and seeing what we can be unburdened by what we have been, we must speak truth. And speak the truth, uncomfortable and difficult though it may be to hear.

The honorees tonight speak the truth. You have spoken the hard truth about unchecked criminal sexual abuse and held a perpetrator accountable and demanded accountability. You have shown so much courage in doing that. You speak the truth about the need for women, and in particular women of color, to be seen and heard and for their stories to be told. From the Senate floor to movie sets to concert stages, you speak the truth. You speak the truth about gun violence that tears our communities apart and takes away our children. From Parkland to Chicago to South Los Angeles, you've been speaking those truths.

You speak the truth about America's history in all of its greatness and in all of its complexity. You have spoken the truth about the right of self-determination for every woman across the globe.

That is what we need at this moment. This is an inflection moment, I believe, in the history of our country. This is a moment where there are powerful voices trying to sow hate and division among us. If we're going to deal with where we are at this inflection moment, we must speak all these truths. One of the most significant and important truths right now is also that the vast majority of us have so much more in common than what separates us. Let's speak and own that truth, in the face of those who are trying to have us point fingers at each other and divide us. Let's speak these truths.

The final point that I'll make is this: In this inflection moment in the history of our country, this is a moment in which, yes, these truths must be spoken. We need to bring folks together. Let's also recognize this moment will pass. At some moment, this will pass. And years from now, people are gonna look in our eyes, each one of us, and they will ask us, "Where were you at that inflection moment?" What we're all going to be able to say is that we were here together, and we were fighting for the best of who we are.

Tyra Banks

Three months after Tyra Banks graduated high school, she "got discovered" as a model. So instead of going to college, the California teen studied the fashion industry like it was an exam, consuming every magazine, book, and runway photograph she could get her hands on. When she started meeting with designers, she learned to change her outfit and makeup to match the fashion house's signature style. The hard work paid off: Banks booked 25 fashion shows for 1991 Paris Fashion Week, her first runway season. "Yeah, I was a 'sensation,'" she told *Glamour*, "but really it was strategy."

Strategy, defined as the art of planning, is how Banks has always navigated her career. When American modeling agencies told her they weren't interested because they "already had a Black girl" in their lineup, she moved to Europe and started her career there. Then, when designers told her she had become "too curvy" to continue modeling, she went where her body would be celebrated and booked the cover of *Sports Illustrated*'s Swimsuit Issue. When Banks later wanted to transition to producing and TV hosting—first with *America's Next Top Model* and then *The Tyra Banks Show*—she was told it would never work. Both series were so successful that *Glamour* awarded her the Woman of the Year Award in 2008 for being "TV's fiercest woman-power icon."

"If you have a dream, you knock on that front door," she said in her acceptance speech. "If they won't allow you in, go through the back door. If the back door is locked, go through the cellar. Or the basement. If that's all boarded up, climb your butt through the window. But *get in*."

Sometimes the way to success is not a straight path—but using strategy, like Banks has proven, will get you where you want to go.

Megan Rapinoe

WOMAN OF THE YEAR 2019

The year Megan Rapinoe was honored as a WOTY, 2019, was a busy one for the U.S. Women's National Soccer Team midfielder. Rapinoe scored the most goals at the World Cup, became the first out gay woman to pose for *Sports Illustrated*'s Swimsuit Issue, and was one of the most vocal leaders in the team's fight for equal pay. All of this—and more—solidified her legacy as an outspoken hero for women's rights on and off the soccer field.

"Winning the World Cup is very difficult—it's arduous, it's a long cycle, it's hard," Rapinoe said at the time. "And then on top of it, we inspired a movement that transcended the sport. Now we have to come home and fight a lawsuit to convince everyone that we're worth a little bit more money? That's bullshit."

The team's request for equal pay, which started long before Rapinoe joined, was frustrating for players and fans alike. "At the crux of everything is that when we play a game—win the game, lose the game, tie the game, whatever—what we're asking is that we'll have the same opportunity to make the same amount of money," Rapinoe explained. "We should be treated equally." And though all members were doing their part to fight for change, Rapinoe became especially known for her made-to-be-memed comments on the subject. At the 2019 FIFA Women's World Cup parade, she implored the crowd to work together to improve their communities. "It's our responsibility to make this world a better place," she said.

And when she took the stage at *Glamour*'s Women of the Year Awards that November, she delivered yet another powerful missive that moved the crowd to its feet, roaring for change. "I want to reimagine what it means to be successful, what it means to have influence, what it means to have power, and what that all looks like," she declared. "We've got to switch the game up. Caring is cool. Lending your platform to others is cool. Sharing your knowledge and your success and your influence and your power is cool. Giving all the fucks is cool. Doing more is cool."

Rapinoe gave us all a rallying cry: "There's so much momentum, but we have to move forward and we have to be better. So everybody: We have to do more. We're here. We're ready."

"In the same breath that I want to be seen for all of the things that have nothing to do with being a woman," Megan Rapinoe told *Glamour* in 2019, "I very much want to be seen as all of these things as a woman."

The 2015 World Cup roster (listed alphabetically): Shannon Boxx, Morgan Brian, Lori Chalupny, Whitney Engen, Ashlyn Harris, Tobin Heath, Lauren Holiday, Julie Johnston, Meghan Klingenberg, Ali Krieger, Sydney Leroux, Carli Lloyd, Alex Morgan, Alyssa Naeher, Kelley O'Hara, Heather O'Reilly, Christen Press, Christie Rampone, Megan Rapinoe, Amy Rodriguez, Becky Sauerbrunn, Hope Solo, Abby Wambach.

The 1999 World Cup roster (not pictured): Michelle Akers, Brandi Chastain, Tracy Ducar, Lorrie Fair, Joy Fawcett, Danielle Fotopoulos, Julie Foudy, Mia Hamm, Kristine Lilly, Shannon MacMillan, Tiffeny Milbrett, Carla Overbeck, Cindy Parlow, Christie Pearce, Tiffany Roberts, Briana Scurry, Kate Sobrero, Tisha Venturini, Saskia Webber, Sara Whalen.

The U.S. Women's National Soccer Team

WOMEN OF THE YEAR 1999 AND 2015

Every single honoree that *Glamour* has celebrated over the years could be described as a game changer—but for the members of the U.S. Women's National Soccer Team (USWNT), that's literally true. They're the most successful women's soccer team in the world, winning four World Cup titles (1991, 1999, 2015, 2019) and four Olympic gold medals (1996, 2004, 2008, 2012). And it's the reason *Glamour* has honored them so often—in 1999 and 2015 after their World Cup wins, and then again with a nod to World Cup high-scorer Megan Rapinoe in 2019. More important, they've shown little girls—and boys—what's truly possible in sports. "Now when [kids] are picking teams at recess, it won't matter anymore if you're a boy or a girl," Brandi Chastain, a defender and midfielder from 1988 to 2004, said of the team's impact in 1999.

For Abby Wambach, a forward from 2003 to 2015 and the team's highest-ever scorer, it goes even further than that. "What we did not only helped the popularity of women's soccer and women's sports in our country, but women, period," she told *Glamour* in 2015. "To be a part of a generation that is pushing the needle forward is something I am very proud of."

For all the team's success, its biggest battle has been for equal pay. Though the USWNT consistently performs better than its male counterpart, the women continue to be paid less. Case in point: When the team won the World Cup in 2015, it earned $2 million in prize money. The men's team, which was eliminated, got $9 million. So in 2016 five players filed a complaint with the Equal Employment Opportunity Commission alleging gender discrimination by U.S. Soccer. By 2019 the whole team had filed a lawsuit against their employers. When the women won that summer's World Cup, the stadium erupted into a timely chant: "Equal pay! Equal pay!"

"I don't remember being informed about the discrimination that girls and women face in sports when I was younger," said Alex Morgan, a forward who made her World Cup debut in 2011. "But now I see eight-year-olds with posters saying, 'Go Alex, thank you for giving me a better future.' I can't wait to share all these stories with my daughter and be able to tell her a little piece of history that mom had to fight for."

2017

2001

Editor in Chief **Cindi Leive**

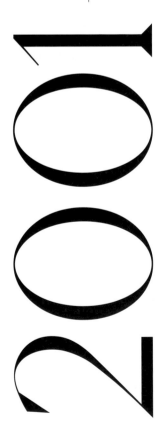

Cindi Leive, editor in chief from 2001 to 2017, from top: pregnant with her first child, and with Lady Gaga, Hillary Clinton, and Tracee Ellis Ross.

I WAS AN EDITORIAL ASSISTANT AT *GLAMOUR* WHEN I attended the first Women of the Year ceremony, in 1990. Ruth Whitney, the editor in chief at the time, presided over the evening. *Glamour* editor Judith Daniels, a pioneering woman in her own right as the founding editor of *Savvy,* had brought the idea of honoring women of achievement to Whitney. And together they developed the first WOTY Awards. Back then there weren't many award ceremonies that brought together women from all these different walks of life. Ruth really resisted the idea of honoring mostly celebrities—she wanted to see politicians, scientists, and women who stood alone in male-dominated fields.

That first year, I was assigned to be an aide. But one of the most high-impact moments came the following year when Anita Hill was honored. She had just testified in front of a very hostile Senate Judiciary Committee less than a month earlier, and Ruth had walked into the office on the Tuesday after and said, "Rip up the Women of the Year story. We're going to be honoring Anita Hill." There were a lot of raised eyebrows in the mainstream media at the time, taking the attitude of "it's a he said, she said thing." Ruth didn't buy that. Her instinct was, "I believe her. We're honoring her, period." I was assigned to write the story, which was incredibly exciting. For me, watching Ruth so forcefully throw herself behind the words of a woman was an early lesson in trusting your gut.

My first WOTY as editor in chief was in 2001—right after September 11, which had so personally affected New York, where the Women of the Year Awards lived. At the ceremony we honored several of the fallen rescue workers and officers. We also honored a group called RAWA, the Revolutionary Association of the Women of Afghanistan, which was dedicated to fighting for human rights and social justice in Afghanistan. It was important we recognized

the American heroes as well as the women who had been fighting and living under extremism for years.

During the 2000s I wanted to honor Hillary Clinton for her work as a U.S. senator. So after she ran for president the first time, in 2008, I went down to Washington, D.C., and parked myself in her office until her head of communications finally relented and said she'd come. It was the most significant run for president a woman had made at that time, and I couldn't imagine WOTY without her there. In 2016, after her second run for president, the awards ceremony was scheduled six days after the election. We all thought we'd be celebrating the first woman president. Instead, we were reckoning with the deep racism and misogyny in our country. We assembled a group of people to pay tribute to Clinton, and Shonda Rhimes wrote a beautiful script that Tracee Ellis Ross and others read onstage. That was a very powerful moment.

One of the groups of people we honored that I look back on most vividly was Alicia Garza, Opal Tometi, and Patrisse Cullors, the three cofounders of Black Lives Matter. They started the movement much earlier than when we honored them, in 2016. We were already late. But their words onstage had such a profound impact, and it was impossible to imagine WOTY without recognizing the incredible work they were doing on behalf of all Americans, Black American women in particular.

There were a lot of glittery celebrity moments too, like the dinner where Julia Roberts got the whole room to sing "Happy Birthday" to her friend Ryan Murphy. Or the time when Lady Gaga teared up as the P.S. 22 Chorus performed her own songs to her onstage at Carnegie Hall. And personal moments: One year my assistant brought her boyfriend to the dinner afterward, and he proposed. Another year, I was on the red carpet in a beautiful borrowed Alexander McQueen dress when a publicist whispered to me in alarm that Karlie Kloss—there to present an award to McQueen creative director/designer Sarah Burton—had just arrived in the same dress. (God bless the amazing, unruffled Karlie. She left, changed, and came right back, all in good humor.)

The fact that *Glamour* honored so many people who were doing significant work was the most important part to me. It was always meaningful to see the level of excitement that women like Jennifer Lopez and Solange Knowles—incredibly accomplished themselves—be inspired by the lesser-known women and watch the bonds that would develop as they met. A lot grew out of the Women of the Year Awards, most emphatically those deep connections between women who supported each other's work, and that's what I'm most proud of.

Maxine Waters

WOMAN OF THE YEAR 2017

When Maxine Waters accepted her 2017 Woman of the Year lifetime achievement award, the audience knew they were in for a *moment*. During her decades-long career, the California congresswoman had been a fearless advocate for underserved people, creating landmark legislation around affirmative action, police reform, and other important issues. Then in 2017, Twitter users noticed that the then 79-year-old progressive politician had a laser-sharp tongue and was happy to deploy it anytime she spotted wrongdoing among her colleagues. When former FBI director James B. Comey testified that he avoided being alone with President Donald Trump, Waters tweeted, "Women across the country can relate."

It reached a high point that summer during a memorable hearing in which she shut down a meandering Treasury Secretary Steven Mnuchin by declaring, repeatedly, that she was "reclaiming my time." By the November WOTY ceremony, the phrase had become a call to action: Speak up. Push back. Reclaim your time.

"You recognize when a leader is irresponsible," Waters said as she took the stage that night. "You recognize when a leader is dishonorable and disrespectful. You recognize when a leader is dangerous. Even if that leader is the President of the United States of America." She then led the crowd in an impassioned chant: "Impeach 45! Impeach 45!"

Waters hoped that moments like that would inspire younger generations to use their voice. "I want young people to know that not only should they speak up for themselves, but sometimes they have to make demands," she said at the time. "I want young people to feel comfortable in their own skin, to like themselves, and to be able to present themselves— whenever and wherever they need to."

Julianne Moore

WOMAN OF THE YEAR 2000

Julianne Moore has played a paleontologist, an FBI agent, a porn star, and even the former governor of Alaska Sarah Palin. "In my career as an actress, I have spent an awful lot of time simply pretending to accomplish things," she said jokingly to *Glamour* in 2000. We respectfully disagree.

Offscreen is a different story—which is why, 10 years after the Women of the Year Awards was created, Moore was honored. By 2000 the actor had already spent the course of her decades-long career speaking up for causes she believed in—gay rights, gun control, gender parity, and, most vocally and repeatedly, women's reproductive rights—at a time when celebrities were encouraged to shy away from topics as polarizing as abortion laws. But the actor was passionate and so vocal about women's rights to choose that she even scored a spot on the board of advocates for Planned Parenthood.

"I don't believe actors need to necessarily be advocates for anything," she told *Glamour* with characteristic humility. "I mean, after all, we are actors. *However*, because I'm a public person, young girls see me. If I can make a difference by talking that way, it's the least I can do."

Of all her causes, reproductive rights was the one she has held most dear. Because, as she explained, "if you don't have reproductive freedom, you have no personal freedom."

"Reproductive rights are really a basic freedom," Julianne Moore told *Glamour*. "And, my God, not to have that choice is stifling!"

Malala Yousafzai at Girls Prep in the Bronx, which named a classroom after the activist.

Malala Yousafzai

WOMAN OF THE YEAR 2013

Malala Yousafzai is named after Malalai, an Afghan warrior who rallied the army for battle against British troops in 1880. It's fitting—Yousafzai is an activist and fighter in every sense of the word, a role she first embraced at age 12. After the Taliban banned girls from attending school in the Swat district of Pakistan, where she lived in 2009, Yousafzai started writing a detailed, albeit anonymous, diary for the BBC Urdu website about her life. (A local journalist had asked her father, a school owner, if he knew of a student willing to write. She was the only one who volunteered.) As she grew in confidence, and despite the risks, she stopped using a pseudonym. This led to her appearance in a *New York Times* documentary, and she began speaking across the country advocating for girls' education. When she met the prime minister of Pakistan in 2011, she had a list of demands ready.

But as her work gained attention, she worried she would become a target. "I used to think that one day the Taliban would come for me," she told *Glamour*. "And I thought, What would I do? I said to myself, Malala, you must be brave. You must not be afraid of anyone. You are only trying to get an education—you are not committing a crime. I would even tell my attacker, 'I want education for your son and daughter.'"

On October 9, 2012, her worries became reality when a young Taliban man shot her three times. She survived the attempted assassination—and became motivated to fight even harder. In the year following the attack, Yousafzai wrote the memoir *I Am Malala* and became one of the youngest Nobel Peace Prize nominees *ever*.

In 2013 she accepted her *Glamour* Woman of the Year Award onstage in New York, telling the audience: "The Taliban showed me they thought that the other girls speaking for their rights would also stop. They thought that they would spread fear, terror, but they failed. I believe that if you are sincere to your own heart, then you can do anything. And I can do anything."

"I believe all wom educated, will see cha

that when
en are
then you
this world
nge."

—MALALA YOUSAFZAI, WOMAN OF THE YEAR 2013

Waris Dirie

WOMAN OF THE YEAR 1998

Somali-born supermodel Waris Dirie always wanted to use her platform for more. She was just five years old when she was subjected to female genital mutilation (FGM), the inhumane practice in which the genitals are partially or entirely removed—often without anesthesia.

A survivor to her core, Dirie ran away from home at 13 years old to escape an arranged marriage to a man at least 60 years old. She eventually landed in London, working hard at McDonald's and living in a YMCA to make ends meet. Her life changed once again, at 18, when a chance meeting with a photographer led to a massively successful career. She appeared in campaigns with everyone from Chanel to Revlon, walked all the major runways in Paris, New York, and Milan, and even starred in a James Bond movie.

But Dirie had another goal in mind—to speak out about the horrors of FGM. In 1998, when *Glamour* honored Dirie as a Woman of the Year, the practice was being performed on an estimated 2 million girls each year. Many, including Dirie's own sister, had died from complications. After Dirie opened up about her past in a groundbreaking interview with *Marie Claire* magazine in 1997, she became a special ambassador for the United Nations, coauthored an acclaimed memoir about her life, and traveled the world speaking out about the horrors of FGM.

Dirie's Desert Flower Foundation, created in 2002, continued her commitment to ending the practice and promoting gender equality globally. According to the World Health Organization, approximately 200 million women have been affected by FGM worldwide. "I have to put my privacy aside," she told *Glamour* in 1998. "What else is more important than saving a child's life?" Twenty-six of the 29 countries in Africa where the practice was still occurring later prohibited it by law or constitutional decree. Because of her bravery, the fight to end FGM continues.

As a United Nations special ambassador, model Waris Dirie has traveled the world lobbying for the elimination of female genital mutilation.

Tammy Duckworth

WOMAN OF THE YEAR 2006

In 2004 the Black Hawk helicopter that Major Ladda "Tammy" Duckworth was piloting during a mission in Iraq was shot down by a rocket-propelled grenade. She lost both her legs in the attack, but Duckworth used her rehabilitation at Walter Reed National Military Medical Center in Washington, D.C., to plot her next move: a career switch into politics. "Four months in bed is a long time to watch politicians make bad decisions on C-SPAN," Duckworth quipped to *Glamour*.

In 2006, the year *Glamour* honored Duckworth as a Woman of the Year, she ran for a seat in the House, representing Illinois on a progressive platform opposing the Iraq war she had served in. Though she lost that campaign, she won a personal war: Her bid had given her—and her platform—a national spotlight. She kept the momentum going by leading the Illinois Department of Veterans Affairs, where she started a program that helped veterans and service members with post-traumatic stress disorder and brain injuries. When she ran again for the House—first in 2012, then in 2014—she won, both times, and continued advocating for disability rights. In 2016 she leveled up and won a Senate seat. During her tenure, she introduced important legislation that made it easier for small businesses to comply with the Americans With Disabilities Act, and to make fitness facilities more accessible. For her work helping the disabled community from the federal level, the American Association of People With Disabilities (AAPD) honored her in 2020 with a legacy award.

For Duckworth, the first woman to take maternity leave while serving in the Senate, this drive to fight for others' rights was more than just a soldier's instinct. "Stand up for what's important to you," she told *Glamour*. "Or someone else will make decisions for you."

Reese Witherspoon

WOMAN OF THE YEAR 2015

By 2012 Reese Witherspoon had gained international fame thanks to her role as Elle Woods in the film *Legally Blonde* and won an Oscar for playing June Carter Cash in *Walk the Line*. But, much like Elle and June, despite her undisputed success she knew she was capable of so much more. She scheduled meetings with several movie studio heads and asked them all the same question: What's in the works for women? Only one was developing a project for a woman lead.

That didn't sit well with Witherspoon, so that year she did something about it, forming her own production company with a focus on creating dynamic roles for women. Loved the film *Gone Girl* and television shows *Big Little Lies* and *Little Fires Everywhere*? They're all blockbuster hits that redefined modern-day notions of sisterhood—and they're all produced by Witherspoon. "I have this drive from my upbringing to be a doer, not just a complainer," she said. "I have achieved a certain amount of success, and I felt a responsibility to my daughter and to women in this world to create more opportunities for women. Women of different ethnicities and socio-economic backgrounds. We're 50 percent of the population. Shouldn't we be in 50 percent of the stories?"

The stories she has developed are all vastly different, but they share a common thread: Women at the center, in all their many complexities. "Women want to see the truth," Witherspoon said. "They don't want to see some perfect girl." She was honored at *Glamour*'s Women of the Year Awards in 2015 after her production company's first two movies, *Wild* and *Gone Girl*, earned more than $400 million at box offices worldwide.

Witherspoon hasn't just put in the work for herself, either—she has continued to create opportunities for women writers, actors, producers, and directors through the projects she has picked. "Men rise through the ranks because of potential, but women have to prove themselves—while trying to have children and having no family leave," she said. "No woman's getting hired because of her potential. I hope that we can invest *more* in female potential."

Behind every Woman of the Year, Reese Witherspoon said, is "a safety net of love, compassion, and encouragement."

"To be co
you have
an army
holdin

urageous,
to have
of people
g you."

—REESE WITHERSPOON, WOMAN OF THE YEAR 2015

Emme

"It's very exciting to be part of a revolution," supermodel Emme said in her 1997 Woman of the Year profile. Indeed it was: As the first plus-size model to achieve massive commercial success, Emme, whose full name is Emme Aronson, was everywhere—in major fashion spreads, serving as a Revlon spokeswoman, appearing on *People* magazine's 50 Most Beautiful People list. These were more than just career wins, though: As a size 14–16, Emme gave visibility to women whose bodies were not a size 0.

"About 60 percent of women wear a size 12 and up," the model said at the time. "I'm advocating an acceptance of that size by our culture and by women whose natural body type varies from the cultural ideal."

Emme also used her platform to connect with women who, like her, struggled with body image. In *True Beauty*, her memoir and self-help book, she revealed that her stepfather had subjected her to weekly weigh-ins and comments about her hips, thighs, and belly. She began a cycle of disordered eating that worsened at 15, when her mother died of cancer. Her relationship with her body changed after she started rowing in college. And when a friend suggested she try modeling in 1988, she listened.

If society can drop its obsession with having the "perfect" body, Emme argued, we could all get so much more out of life. Unfortunately, almost three decades after her WOTY win, there is still much work to do. But Emme did help pave the way for models like Gabi Gregg (a.k.a. Gabi Fresh) and Ashley Graham to take the body-positive movement to even greater heights in the new millennium. The revolution she started continues through them.

Emme was the first plus-size model to be the face of Revlon.

Manal al-Sharif

WOMAN OF THE YEAR 2018

It's something millions of women around the world have done hundreds—no, probably thousands—of times, and almost certainly without attributing it any huge significance: get into a car, put it into drive, and *go*. But that was not a freedom women in Saudi Arabia could enjoy until June 24, 2018, when the kingdom finally declared that women could drive a car without a male guardian present.

It was a bittersweet victory for Manal al-Sharif, who helped launch the Women2Drive campaign in 2011 and, in order to gain support, posted a viral video of herself driving illegally, for which she was arrested. (That didn't stop her. She was detained again and spent nine days in jail.) Though the ban was lifted in 2018, she had already left the country for a self-imposed exile in Australia. It wasn't an easy decision—she had to leave her son, Aboudi, in custody with his father. As of 2018, Aboudi, then 13, had still not met his brother, Daniel, from al-Sharif's second marriage. She said she hopes that one day Aboudi will understand why she had to speak up—and what it cost her. "Eventually," she told *Glamour* in her WOTY interview, "he will know."

She has continued fighting for equality, even from a distance, speaking out about the country's punitive guardianship laws, which require women to have permission from a man to do basic things like go to school. "A Saudi woman is stripped away from all her rights, her face, name, and identity," she told *Glamour*. "And yet she is there. She is a survivor; she's a fighter. She makes it against all the odds."

Oral Lee Brown

WOMAN OF THE YEAR 2002

In 1987 a chance encounter on a side street turned California realtor Oral Lee Brown into a truly extraordinary advocate and mentor for dozens of underserved students—one with a charitable foundation that continues to this day.

Brown was standing on a street corner in East Oakland, California, waiting for the light to change, when a young girl, about eight years old, approached her and asked, "Lady, would you give me a quarter?"

Brown did more than that—she bought the child bologna, cheese, and bread for her family. When she asked the girl if she went to school, the girl shrugged and replied, "Sometimes." The answer stuck with Brown, who felt compelled to do whatever she could to help Oakland's kids. A few weeks later she turned up at her local elementary school and proposed a deal: She would adopt a class of 23 first graders and pay for college for anyone who graduated high school in 1999.

Brown's salary wouldn't be enough to keep her promise—she was earning $45,000 at the time—but she was determined. She cut down on expenses, set aside $10,000 of her own income each year, and invested wisely. While those moves got her closer to her goal, she also worked tirelessly to organize massive charity fundraisers to reach the finish line. Altogether she brought in more than $1 million over the years. When 19 of the 23 kids graduated, Brown paid for their college education. In 2002, when *Glamour* honored her as Woman of the Year, she was on her third phase of students.

By 2017 her local foundation was on its seventh phase of students, bringing the total to more than 136 young people whom she'd helped with mentoring, tutoring, and financial support. "It's hard at times," she told *Glamour* of the commitment, "but the important thing is that I don't abandon these kids like so many other people in their lives have. When I was younger I realized that education is everything. It gives you choices. I'm grateful I can offer my kids those choices."

Oral Lee Brown with five of the students she helped put through college.

"Life is short and tomorrow is not promised," Viola Davis told *Glamour* in 2018. "And at some point you have to enjoy the fruits of your labor."

Viola Davis

WOMAN OF THE YEAR 2018

Viola Davis's gripping film and television performances over three decades launched her into a global spotlight. Whether it was her portrayal of tough-as-nails lawyer Annalise in the long-running legal drama *How to Get Away With Murder* or her turn as nurturing housewife Rose in the play turned film *Fences*, in each of her roles—in *all* that she took on—Davis got to the heart of the character, pulling out what makes them most human.

In 2017 Davis achieved the triple crown of acting: She became one of only 23 actors since 1953 to have won a competitive Tony Award (in Davis's case, two, for *King Hedley II* in 2001 and *Fences* in 2010), a Primetime Emmy (for *How to Get Away With Murder* in 2015), and an Oscar (*Fences*, 2017).

For Davis, her upbringing as the first Black family to move into the working-class neighborhood of Central Falls, Rhode Island, not only gave her empathy but also inspired her ambitions. "My past has forged who I was gonna become because I had it hard," she told *Glamour*. Growing up poor—*really poor,* she explained—meant she felt invisible. Even when she did experience a breakthrough, like attending the elite acting institution Juilliard in the early '90s, the theater scene was not an inclusive, safe place for a Black actor with a voice. "Because I came from sort of nothing, I had to build my life myself, and I realized I was never gonna be given the opportunities that I felt was worthy of my talent and my potential."

It wasn't easy in an industry where art did not imitate life. "It became very, very obvious that I had to be the change that I wanted to see," she said. "Back in the day, people told actors to study life. And it is not life when you see every single movie with the exact same people in them."

She wanted more—so she achieved it. "I wanted to create a legacy," she said. "I wanted to create a change where I saw people of color who were included in the narrative in Hollywood because I'd been told that someone who looks exactly like me—someone who has a wide nose, wide lips, darker than a paper bag—is wrong.... To see someone like me, it opens the door to this whole world, imagination, dreams, vision that I can have for my life."

That push to inspire young people to "dream big and dream fierce" is why *Glamour* honored her in 2018. As she put it in her profile interview, "I always say I'm allowing the eight-year-old chocolate girl from Central Falls to look at the awesome woman she gets to become."

Constance McMillen

WOMAN OF THE YEAR 2010

Constance McMillen didn't set out to change the world in 2010—she just wanted to go to prom with her girlfriend. They planned to wear tuxes. But when the vice principal at Itawamba Agricultural High School in Fulton, Mississippi, found out, he told McMillen the teens couldn't come as a couple.

McMillen, then 18, was raised to be proud of who she was. So, with the support of her family, she called the American Civil Liberties Union. The reaction was extreme: Now faced with a lawsuit, the school board canceled the event altogether. The story became national news, and McMillen was flooded with messages of support from the LGBTQ+ community. But inside her high school, things were different. Angry about losing their dance, McMillen's classmates reacted with protest signs and T-shirts that read "No prom" on the front and "Thanks Constance" on the back. She even lost her best friend.

"I didn't want everyone to hate me," McMillen told *Glamour* later that year. "But sometimes you got to do what you got to do. The easiest way is not always the best way."

That November she was honored as a Woman of the Year for her bravery. And since she couldn't wear a tuxedo to prom, designer Isaac Mizrahi made one just for her for the ceremony. "After everything that I went through just because I stood up for what I believe in, stuff like this really makes it worth it," she shared with the crowd after a standing ovation. "My message to everyone here: You should just stand up for what you believe in and just ignore the consequences because you're going to make a change. If you think something is wrong, stand up and do something about it."

In the following years McMillen continued to support LGBTQ+ rights—but for her, the movement was much bigger than any one person. "I don't care if people know my name or know who I am," she said in 2010, "as long as they know there was a girl that did stand up."

Constance McMillen, photographed in her childhood bedroom in Fulton, Mississippi, in 2010.

Judge Rosemarie Aquilina

WOMAN OF THE YEAR 2018

As *Glamour* spotlighted in her 2018 Woman of the Year profile, Rosemarie Aquilina is no ordinary judge. In a system that often favors process and protocol over emotion, Aquilina turned her courtroom into something relatively unheard of at the time: a safe environment for survivors of former USA Gymnastics doctor Larry Nassar's sexual abuse to have a voice. During the weeklong sentencing hearing for Nassar, the Michigan circuit court judge gave ample time and space for all the "sister survivors," as she called the women whom he had abused, to have the floor as part of his guilty plea deal. More than 150 came forward with impact statements. Some were public, others anonymous—but all explained in devastating detail the pain and trauma that Nassar had caused.

Aquilina was praised for her seemingly revolutionary victim-centered approach to the courtroom, but the judge told *Glamour* that in her 14 years on the bench, she's always wanted to create a safe space. "When you ask, 'What would you like me to know?' it empowers [people]," Aquilina told *Glamour* in her WOTY profile. "They go, 'Someone's listening; let me talk now.'"

And in January 2018, after all the victim statements were read, Aquilina finally shared her own voice: "I've just signed your death warrant," she famously told Nassar after sentencing him up to 175 years. "You've done nothing to deserve to walk outside a prison again."

Some judges criticized Aquilina for speaking harshly, but she didn't see it that way. "It's the people's court; it's our laws, our community," she said. "It's our Constitution."

The Sister Army That Took Down Larry Nassar

WOMEN OF THE YEAR 2018

It took more than 150 survivors, a determined detective, a dedicated attorney, and an impassioned judge to get former USA Gymnastics doctor Larry Nassar finally behind bars. This Sister Army of extraordinary heroes stopped a cycle of abuse that lasted more than 20 years, and in the process they told the world: Believe women.

Eighty-four survivors came together at Michigan's Supreme Court Building, also known as the Hall of Justice. Pictured on the balcony (all in alphabetical order): Selena Brennan, Devin Carapellucci, Lisa Marie Dearing, Katherine Gordon, Amanda Hancock, Melissa Hudecz, Morgan McCaul, Alexis Moore, Chloe Myers, Eve Petrie, Erin Poliquin, Gabriela Ralph, Heidi Scott, Katelyn Skrabis, Nicole Soos, Marta Stern, Morgan Valley, Kourtney Weidner, Lindsay Woolever.

Pictured on the ground floor: Six women who choose to remain anonymous, Sarah Allen, Presley Allison, Alexis Alvarado, Gwen Anderson, Christina Ball, Christina Barba, Amanda Barterian, Heather Berry, Autumn Blaney, Alexandra Bourque, Larissa Boyce, Elizabeth Brady, Ashley Bremer, Jade Capua, Suma Cherukuri, Katie Clevenger, Savannah Coomer, Amanda Cosman, Elena Cram, Rachael Denhollander, Jaime Doski, Ashley Erickson, Megan Farnsworth, Grace French, Lyndsy Gamet, Leslie Givens, Trinea Gonczar, Louise Harder, Natalie Hawkins, Annette Hill, Lisa Hovey, Kara Johnson, Kathleen Lovellette, Heidi Lutz, Tiffany Mack, Katherine Mahon, Chelsey Markham (who died by suicide; she is pictured in the photo held by her mother, Donna), Lindsay Medrano, Emma Ann Miller, Danielle Moore, Jenelle Moul, Amy Place, Aly Raisman, Breanne Ranta, Alexandra Romano, Jessica Schedler, Amanda Smith, Kayla Spicher, Taylor Stevens, Jillian Swinehart, Amanda Thomashow, Melody van der Veen, Olivia Venuto, Mimi Wegener, Helena Weick, Ashleigh Weiszbrod, Isabelle Wittebort, Chelsea Zerfas.

Nicole Kidman

WOMAN OF THE YEAR 2008 AND 2017

Over the course of her career, Nicole Kidman has won more Oscars, Emmys, and Golden Globes than most actors can ever dream of—eight in total. But when she took the stage to accept her 2008 Woman of the Year Award for her activism efforts with the United Nations Development Fund for Women (UNIFEM), she didn't reflect on her already massively successful career, the lineup of talented directors she had worked with, or the fact that she was one of the highest-paid stars in Hollywood. Instead, she offered some wisdom on a subject virtually all women can relate to: the pressure to have it all.

"A lot of people seem to ask women, 'Can you have it all?'" she said. "I don't believe that you can. I believe you can have balance.... I think you can have your dreams, and you can have an extraordinary career, but try and achieve balance in your life." She touched on this topic again when she won in 2017, this time for her nuanced portrayal of a domestic abuse survivor in HBO's smash-hit *Big Little Lies*. As Kidman took the stage, she praised her family and husband Keith Urban for their continued "good love." "Because as much as I'm a strong woman," she explained, "I need help and I need support."

That craving for balance was what led Kidman to her important work with UNIFEM, which she joined as a goodwill ambassador in 2006. "We didn't call her; she called us," Joan Libby Hawk, UNIFEM's former chief of public affairs, told *Glamour* in 2008. "And she said, 'I'm in this for the long haul.' There's a level of passion that shows."

This involvement included visits to shelters for domestic abuse survivors across the world, from Switzerland to Kosovo, long before she played Celeste in *Big Little Lies* (produced by fellow WOTY winner Reese Witherspoon). "The accumulation of experience gives you a debt in terms of compassion," Kidman said. "I am very fortunate, and I feel dedicated to giving back to other women. Wherever I am now, I make sure I visit a women's shelter. But I don't want to do it in a frivolous way."

That passion for activism has extended to her career too, most notably when she made a public pledge in 2017 to work with women directors at least every 18 months. "As an actor you're only as good as the things you're offered. And there just weren't any women offering me things," she said. "So when you dissect that, you realize there aren't women offering you things because they don't have the opportunities. I work to raise money for women's cancers; I use my voice for violence against women. And so I was like, I need to be part of the movement that will, hopefully, change the statistics in my field."

It took time, but Kidman finally found a balance that worked for her. And if that ever falters, she said it won't stay that way for long: "Even if your wings get clipped, you can build them back and you can fly."

In her 2008 Woman of the Year speech, Nicole Kidman shared this wisdom: "Get involved, keep challenging the status quo, and you don't need to conform because rebellion creates character. Very important."

"Learn no, bu no fe sayin

to say
t have
ar in
g yes."

—NICOLE KIDMAN, WOMAN OF THE YEAR 2008 AND 2017

The U.S. Olympic Women's Basketball Team

WOMEN OF THE YEAR 1996

There was more than a gold medal at stake for the 1996 U.S. Olympic women's basketball team. That April the NBA Board of Governors had just approved the concept of the Women's National Basketball Association (WNBA) to launch the following year. All eyes were on the Atlanta games—and the team. If they won they could settle any doubt that women's basketball was a viable professional-league sport.

The team—Teresa Edwards, Ruthie Bolton, Sheryl Swoopes, Lisa Leslie, Katrina McClain, Dawn Staley, Jennifer Azzi, Carla McGhee, Katy Steding, Rebecca Lobo, Venus Lacy, and Nikki McCray—more than rose to the occasion, winning all eight of its games. In the final they dominated with a 111–87 victory over Brazil for the gold. Players like Lisa Leslie and Sheryl Swoopes became instant stars. The WNBA was a go—and *Glamour* honored the team at that year's Women of the Year Awards for its transformation of professional women's sports.

There was still a long way to go—in early 2020, WNBA players were still fighting for equal pay—but the 1996 team paved the way for countless women athletes. "When I was 12, there wasn't a girls' basketball team," Leslie said in 2010, when she was honored again as a Woman of the Year following her retirement from the L.A. Sparks. "The boys wouldn't throw me the ball. But when they finally realized I could shoot very well, even the parents would be like, 'Give it to the girl! Give it to the girl!'" The team's legacy lives on in every young girl who takes up sports.

Members of the 1996 U.S. Olympic team, from left: Ruthie Bolton, Sheryl Swoopes, Jennifer Azzi, Lisa Leslie, Carla McGhee, Katy Steding, and Katrina McClain.

Judy Blume

WOMAN OF THE YEAR 2004

For many young women, reading a Judy Blume book is a rite of passage. Her young adult novels—classics like *Are You There God? It's Me, Margaret* and *Deenie*—have sold more than 85 million copies worldwide. More important, they were some of the first to openly discuss real issues young women face: sexuality, bullying, and birth control among them. But Blume's frank depictions of these so-called taboo topics have also led to her becoming one of the most censored authors in America by conservative groups. On the American Library Association's list of the 100 most challenged books of the 1990s, five of Blume's novels are listed.

For Blume, that was encouragement to keep going. "Censors are afraid of the truth," she said. "The best writing is fearless." The backlash also inspired a new passion for Blume: advocating for literary freedom. Since the 1980s she's worked with the National Coalition Against Censorship to champion authors' rights and fight against book banning. In 2004, the year *Glamour* recognized her work with a WOTY Award, she received the National Book Foundation's Medal for Distinguished Contribution to American Letters, a prestigious honor that celebrates individuals who have made a major cultural contribution to literature.

"Did I plan to become an activist?" she said as she accepted her WOTY Award. "No, but things happen. You either take action or you don't. Standing up and speaking out, you find out, makes you feel a lot better than doing nothing. And while you're doing it, you also find out you're not as alone as you thought you were."

"I never dreamed I'd be standing here tonight," Judy Blume said as she accepted her Woman of the Year Award in 2004. "But then again I never dreamed that my books would become a target of the censors."

Victoria Beckham

WOMAN OF THE YEAR 2015

Victoria Beckham was first introduced to the world as Posh Spice, the most glamorous member of the Spice Girls. So when Beckham made the career change from pop superstar to fashion designer in 2008, many scoffed. A celebrity line is one thing—breaking into the notoriously competitive world of high-end fashion is another. Beckham herself understood the skepticism, though she wasn't deterred. "Nothing ever came naturally to me," she said. "I was never the cleverest, never best at anything. But we always tell our children that if you work hard and believe in yourself, you can do what you want."

Beckham wanted to be taken seriously as a designer, so she launched her line with a low-key presentation given only to industry insiders, an unexpectedly humble (and savvy) move that impressed the fashion elite. Her hard work paid off. In 2011 Beckham's meticulous designs earned her label Designer Brand of the Year at the Fashion Awards. *Glamour* honored her in 2015 for this inspiring role reversal, and since then she has added a namesake makeup and beauty range to her brand as well as a collaboration with sportswear giant Reebok.

"I did have to find myself and my confidence," she said. The key was focusing on what was most important: the women she was designing for. "I want to make other women feel like the best version of themselves. That's the same message as the Spice Girls. It's still Girl Power."

Donna Dees-Thomases

WOMAN OF THE YEAR 2000

In August 1999, just a few months after the Columbine massacre when two 12th-graders murdered 12 students and one teacher, a white supremacist opened fire on a day camp at a California Jewish community center. For Donna Dees-Thomases, a mom of two girls in suburban New Jersey, enough was enough. For 10 months she used every free hour in her day to organize the Million Mom March, a grassroots mobilization of mothers against gun violence whose name was inspired by the 1995 Million Man March for civil rights. Her call for action was heard: On Mother's Day 2000, she and more than 750,000 people from around the United States protested at the nation's capital for stricter gun laws.

"Million Mom March was a grassroots group of women, many of whom had never organized so much as a carpool before," Dees-Thomases told *Glamour* in 2020, two decades after she was nominated as a WOTY. "But they found inner strength, used their talents and their ability to stand up to the gun lobby, and say, 'This is what we're doing.'"

In the years following the Million Mom March, Dees-Thomases has shared her experience and on-the-ground findings with like-minded organizations like March for Our Lives and the Coalition to Stop Gun Violence. The collaboration is needed: In 2018, when March for Our Lives was formed, the gun lobby in the United States was as strong as ever, and mass shootings were so prevalent that more than 4.1 million students in the country's schools had participated in a lockdown or lockdown drills.

"We represent the majority of the country," she told *Glamour* in 2000. "It's time that the laws caught up."

Donna Dees-Thomases, a mother of two girls, organized the Million Mom March in 2000 to protest gun violence.

Anita Hill is the only *Glamour* Woman of the Year to be honored two years in a row.

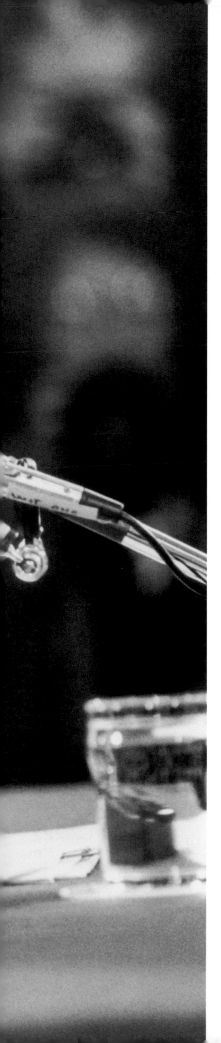

Anita Hill

WOMAN OF THE YEAR 1991 AND 1992

In 1991, young law professor Anita Hill testified before the Senate Judiciary Committee that Clarence Thomas, her supervisor at the Department of Education and the Equal Employment Opportunity Commission, had repeatedly sexually harassed her and was unsuitable to sit on the United States Supreme Court. It took extraordinary bravery to come forward—and even more to get through the hearing. For hours Hill was grilled by an all-white, all-male committee (led by then chairman of the Senate Judiciary Committee Joe Biden) about every excruciating detail of her harassment, only to have her reputation and credibility called into question by Thomas's supporters.

The outcome was not one she had hoped for: Thomas was confirmed. (He continues to serve on the court as of summer 2020.) For her unflinching courage to sacrifice her privacy in order to speak up, *Glamour* honored her as a Woman of the Year, not just in 1991, but again for a special recognition award in 1992—the only honoree to have been recognized consecutively.

Her testimony was a watershed. By 1992, 81 percent of Fortune 500 companies had harassment-awareness programs, and she is credited with inspiring a number of women to run for Senate so that none would ever have to face the line of questioning she did. In the years that followed, complaints filed with the Equal Employment Opportunity Commission more than doubled, new legislation was passed to protect employees from workplace harassment, and private companies across the country started incorporating sexual harassment education into their training programs.

These changes uplifted Hill—and inspired her to keep speaking out. Over the years Hill wrote numerous articles and books on race and gender rights, appeared on programs like *60 Minutes* and *Meet the Press* to advocate for equality, and in 2017 was selected to lead the Commission on Sexual Harassment and Advancing Equality in the Workplace after the #MeToo movement had exposed the widespread sexual assault issues in nearly every industry. "After years of not trusting our own inner voices, we need to say this out loud: Women are entitled to work in places free of sexual harassment," she said at *Glamour*'s 2017 Women of the Year Awards.

Though Hill's testimony did not stop Thomas's confirmation, it led to something far bigger. "I am hopeful that others who may have suffered sexual harassment will not become discouraged by my experience," she said in her 1991 profile interview, "but instead will find the strength to speak up." And they have.

Betty Reid Soskin

WOMAN OF THE YEAR 2018

"What gets remembered is determined by who is in the room doing the remembering," said Betty Reid Soskin, park ranger, civil rights activist, and author of the memoir *Sign My Name to Freedom*.

In 2018, when Soskin was honored as a *Glamour* Woman of the Year, she was one of the people doing the remembering. At 97, Soskin was the oldest person still serving as a permanent National Park Service ranger, and her role, among other duties, included thrice-weekly talks about American history. But not the typical stuff found in textbooks: Soskin educated her audience with the forgotten stories of generations of women of color and other marginalized communities. "History has been written by people who got it wrong," she told *Glamour* in her profile, "but the people who are always trying to get it right have prevailed. If that were not true, I would still be a slave like my great-grandmother."

At the 2018 WOTY Awards, in front of a reverent crowd, Soskin offered even more of her signature wisdom. "The period that I have been most marked by was that of the '60s, where I was an activist in the Black revolution," she said. "Along with millions of others in this country, I helped to create the future I'm privileged to now be living in." Democracy, she reminded the audience, has been experiencing these periods of chaos since 1776—and it's in these periods that democracy is redefined. And by helping us remember the past, Soskin has, in turn, forever shaped our future.

"I'VE LEARNED I DON'T NEED ANSWERS—THE QUESTIONS ARE JUST AS IMPORTANT."

Betty Reid Soskin lived through the Great Depression, World War II, and the civil rights movement of the 1960s. But at 98 years old, she had never before experienced anything like 2020. As the United States prepared for another election year, the coronavirus pandemic had the world in its grip and thousands of lives were lost to the virus.

Then, that summer, an uprising against systemic racism emerged: After George Floyd and Breonna Taylor were killed by police, hundreds of thousands of people gathered around the country to fight for justice and the dismantling of centuries-old oppression. "Things are so much in turmoil right now that everything is going to change significantly," Soskin told Glamour that June. "I don't think I've lived a comparable period. This has all the earmarks of being monumental."

Here she reflects on her 10 decades of life and shares her advice for future generations.

WHAT YOU BELIEVE IS POSSIBLE WILL CHANGE—AND GROW—WITH TIME.

"I've lived my entire life never daring to have any ambitions worth the time to make them 'real.' But in looking back, it occurs to me that these ambitions weren't secondary. They were all top drawer—each with dreams and a life of their own. I suppose the fact that I'm at the end of life, being 98, causes me to have a skewed look at things. Having lived my days out, having met all of my marks, means that I'm more ready than most. I've lived out all my dreams, but I'm still as anxious as ever to see tomorrow. Its promise is still trembling with immediacy and glowing with unexpected joy."

UNDERSTAND WHAT IT IS YOU'RE REALLY SEARCHING FOR.

"Getting in touch with your own truth—and understanding that it's different for everyone—will help you gain confidence. I've learned I don't need to find answers; the questions are just as important. I know now that I'm going to die without answers, but they were never where my attention should have been."

ALWAYS HAVE HOPE ABOUT WHAT'S TO COME, EVEN IN TIMES OF DARKNESS.

"I don't think I'll live to see much change that I haven't already seen. But the fact that I'm still here gives me hope about the future. I know that life is lived in the collective—that my successor is in the collective—and that she or he will pick up where I left off. Nancy Pelosi, at this point in history, is going to be pivotal for the future. She is providing critical leadership at a time when it is most needed."

BUT EMBRACE PERIODS OF CHANGE.

"I think the '60s was when the most important questions in the world were being defined— much more so than the decades that followed. It's when I would have been changed most. I think 2020 will be one of those periods again. It's too early to know what's going to come of it, and I'm not sure where it's going to lead us, but maybe that's what is so exciting about it."

LEADERS & PIONEERS

These barrier breakers fought their way to the top, carved new paths (on this planet and beyond), and taught us that anything really is possible.

Simone Biles

WOMAN OF THE YEAR 2016

Simone Biles is the most decorated gymnast in World Championship history, the kind of athlete who makes headlines every time she breaks yet *another* record.

After her first Olympic event in 2016, a then 19-year-old Biles was already coming home as the most decorated U.S. gymnast in history, with a haul of four gold medals and one bronze that year. It was a moment she had been preparing for since she was six, when her grandmother, who raised her, enrolled Biles in gymnastics lessons. Her raw talent caught the eye of a coach, and the rest is, well, literally athletic history.

The only person Biles is really competing with is herself, and that means putting in the work. In 2012, before starting high school, she made the decision to homeschool so she could focus on training twice a day. "We're out there for less than 10 minutes, and you prepare your whole life for this," she told *Glamour* in 2016 following her Olympic victory. "I can only control what I do, not what anyone else wants me to do. You just have to go out and have fun with it."

Every time she wins or breaks a new record—which is often, including with a gravity-defying triple-double dismount in 2020—she allows herself to feel the victory. "When you stand up there on the podium, and the national anthem is playing, it's surreal," she said. "And then you realize all your hard work has paid off."

Biles's impact extends far beyond gold medals. After it was revealed that former USA Gymnastics doctor Larry Nassar had been sexually abusing his patients for years, Biles was one of more than a hundred women who came forward in 2018 to share that she too was a survivor. "I'm strong, I'll get through it, but it's hard," she told reporters at the time.

Her bravery, on and off the beam, continues to inspire. As of 2019 the gymnast had four incredible moves—and counting—named after her, meaning that her contribution to the sport will remain long after she's retired from the mat. For Biles that's just part of the job. "I'd rather regret the risk that didn't work out than the chances I didn't take at all."

"I've been brought up to never take anything for granted and to always be the best Simone—the best version of myself," Simone Biles told *Glamour* in 2016.

Supreme Court Justice Ruth Bader Ginsburg

WOMAN OF THE YEAR 1993 AND 2012

"The judiciary is not a profession that ranks very high among the glamorously attired," Ruth Bader Ginsburg quipped as she accepted her Woman of the Year lifetime achievement award in 2012. In fact when Ginsburg was nominated to the Supreme Court in 1993, she and fellow justice Sandra Day O'Connor, the only other woman on the bench, had to find creative ways to style their robes because the garments had been designed with men's trouser pockets and ties in mind. Having added sewn-in pockets and lace collars, Ginsburg asked, "Is it not a wonderful sign of progress?"

Of course, Ginsburg's impact on the judiciary goes far beyond sartorial updates. Even before she became a Supreme Court justice, Ginsburg had a long career advocating for gender equality. Despite graduating first in her class at Columbia Law School, she was refused a job with a prominent male judge because she was a woman. Eventually, she was hired as a law professor at Rutgers University, but even then she had to fight to get equal pay. So Ginsburg took it upon herself to create change through what she knew best: the legal system. As a cofounder of the Women's Rights Project at the American Civil Liberties Union, Ginsburg won five of the six cases she argued before the Supreme Court and was famously strategic in the cases she took. (Like taking on cases of male plaintiffs in order to demonstrate to male judges that gender discrimination is harmful to *all*.) A senior leader of the court's liberal wing, Ginsburg was the first Supreme Court justice to officiate a same-sex marriage, and her fiery and impassioned dissents earned her the nickname "The Notorious R.B.G."—a reference to the late rapper The Notorious B.I.G.—and a memorable, loving portrayal by Kate McKinnon on *Saturday Night Live*.

In September 2020, at 87 years old, Ginsburg died due to complications from metastatic pancreatic cancer. Her strength and commitment to decency and fairness were present in her final words to the public, dictated in a statement to her granddaughter: "My most fervent wish is that I will not be replaced until a new president is installed."

"I come from a world where women were protected out of everything," she told *Glamour* when she was first nominated for a Woman of the Year Award, in 1993. "Protected out of being lawyers, out of being engineers, out of being bartenders." But Ginsburg didn't need protection. She needed a new world, so she set about making one.

Jennifer Lopez

WOMAN OF THE YEAR 1999 AND 2011

Jennifer Lopez is often called a triple threat, a title given only to some of the most talented performers in Hollywood, but even that does not encompass all that she has achieved throughout her successful decades-long career. Lopez has topped the box office (*Selena, Hustlers*), the charts ("Love Don't Cost a Thing"), and the small screen (*American Idol*). Her Super Bowl performance with Shakira in 2020 attracted more viewers than the game itself. When she was growing up in the Bronx, neighbors would call her the Supernova. Which raises the question: Is there anything Lopez can't do?

"I'm very comfortable with being productive," she told *Glamour* in 2011. (Lopez has accomplished so much, she's one of only a handful who have been awarded Woman of the Year twice—in 1999 for breaking through with her first chart-topping single, then in 2011 for *American Idol.*) "I like doing things, and I like creating things."

But "doing things" is an understatement when it comes to Lopez—actor, businesswoman, dancer, and producer are just a few of the items on her résumé. "Jennifer's uniqueness lies in her combination of extraordinary beauty, intelligence, and street smarts," her *Monster-in-Law* costar Jane Fonda told *Glamour* in 2011. "She's a fantastic role model. She *owns* it."

Something else J.Lo owns: supreme confidence. It's a quality necessary to be as pioneering as the multi-hyphenate, and something she hopes will inspire other women to chase their own dreams. As she told *Glamour* readers, "You cannot doubt yourself…. You just have to know who you are and what you stand for."

When it comes to work, Jennifer Lopez told *Glamour* in 2011, it's important not to take career ebbs and flows too seriously. "You have to kind of ride the waves, and sometimes you even fall under the water."

"Value y
and
that you'
every

ourself
know
re worth
thing."

—JENNIFER LOPEZ, WOMAN OF THE YEAR 1999 AND 2011

Nancy Pelosi

WOMAN OF THE YEAR 2002 AND 2007

When Nancy Pelosi was elected the House minority whip by her fellow Democrats in 2002, the vote made her the highest-ranking woman in Congress...ever. Pelosi was excited, naturally—but the victory was driven home for her when she attended her first leadership meeting at the White House. As she entered the landmark building, she realized it was the first time in the country's history that a woman had sat at that particular table. "I was not alone," she said in 2002. "I felt surrounded by every woman who ever worked to promote the right to vote for women, to promote women in politics or in professions."

Pelosi reached a more significant milestone in 2007 when she became the Speaker of the House and accepted her second WOTY. That moment also marked the first time a woman had held the position, and Pelosi hoped it would inspire younger generations.

"I hope that in my work in Congress, I will be a role model to some and that I will also pave the way for other young women to take the steps necessary to get us to have a woman president," she told *Glamour*.

She remained in the role until 2011, when Republicans gained control of the House, but was reelected after the 2018 midterms—making her the first former Speaker to return to the post in over 60 years. As second in the line of succession to the presidency, Pelosi has been a key leader amid an increasingly divisive political landscape.

Her advice: "You can accomplish whatever you set out to do if you are prepared," she explained. "Know your power, follow your passion, and without losing faith I know that you will succeed." In other words, just go for it.

"Every generation has a responsibility to make the future better for the next," Nancy Pelosi said as she accepted her 2002 Woman of the Year Award.

Gloria Steinem for *Glamour*, 1964, and in her New York City apartment in 2011.

Gloria Steinem

WOMAN OF THE YEAR 2011

Oprah Winfrey, an icon in her own right, summed up Gloria Steinem's impact on women's rights and reproductive freedom perfectly: "Gloria Steinem is a trailblazer and a pioneer to me and to everybody who spells their name W-O-M-A-N."

Years before she reshaped the narrative of an entire generation, Steinem was a freelance writer living in New York City. The seeds were there even in her early pieces, including one for *Glamour* titled "The Student Princess (or How to Seize Power on the Campus of Your Choice)." But Steinem said things didn't really click for her until she covered an abortion hearing in 1969 for *New York* magazine (she herself had had an abortion at 22, when they were still illegal). Within a few years, she had helped launch the feminist-themed *Ms.* magazine, cofounded the National Women's Political Caucus, and become the first woman to speak at the National Press Club. As her influence grew, her smart one-liners ("The truth will set you free," she once said, "but first it will piss you off") and think pieces ("If Men Could Menstruate," 1978) went viral before going viral was even a thing. The author of seven books, Steinem has campaigned relentlessly for equal, civil, and LGBTQ+ rights and remains a figurehead in the feminist movement today. In 2011 *Glamour* gave her a long-overdue lifetime achievement award for all the progress she had made and continued to fight for.

Though we don't have full gender parity yet, Steinem has hope for the future. "Young women today are more shit-free than we were, much more likely to say what they think," she said. So how do they get started? "Whatever you want to do, do it *now*."

Shonda Rhimes

WOMAN OF THE YEAR 2007

Olivia Pope, Washington, D.C.'s best fixer. Meredith Grey, chief of general surgery at Grey Sloan Memorial Hospital. Annalise Keating, high-profile criminal defense attorney and respected law professor. Only someone as powerful as writer, producer, and creator Shonda Rhimes could dream up such influential and awe-inspiring characters—women so culture-defining that Robin Roberts, a 2014 Woman of the Year, said she watched them with gratitude. "The characters that she puts on television every Thursday night…" Roberts said in 2014, "I just put my shoulders back and go, 'Yeah, thank you.'"

These programs—*Scandal, Grey's Anatomy, How to Get Away With Murder*—dominated ABC's Thursday-night lineup for years thanks to Rhimes's signature blend of high-stakes drama, clever dialogue, and poignant character work. When she won the WOTY in 2007, *Grey's* had been on for four seasons and was the height of must-see TV. By 2020 the series had 16 seasons and counting and remained one of the highest-rated shows.

Creating everything that is Shondaland, as Rhimes's production company is called, requires more than expert storytelling. It needs a savvy businesswoman—a leader on the set and off. "Shonda walks into the room, and I just see possibility," said Chandra Wilson, who plays Dr. Miranda Bailey on *Grey's*. So did Netflix: In 2017 Rhimes signed a multiyear production deal with the streaming service reported to be worth $150 million.

"The possibilities are limitless," Rhimes said. "If you spend your time staring at the obstacles, all you're going to see are the obstacles. Point your finger at the horizon, and run toward it."

Shonda Rhimes on the set of *Grey's Anatomy* in 2007.

"REMEMBER, SUCCESS DOES NOT HAPPEN IMMEDIATELY."

When Shonda Rhimes became the showrunner of Grey's Anatomy, *she set herself a challenge: to uncover what it really means to lead by asking every successful woman she met. Here's what she learned.*

IT TOOK A LONG TIME FOR ME TO FEEL successful. I felt unsteady and unsure, like everything could end at any moment, for years—I think until, maybe, season 10 of *Grey's Anatomy*. I wouldn't call this feeling impostor syndrome, because impostor syndrome is feeling like you don't belong or deserve to be there. I didn't feel that way. But people who sit back and go, "I've made it," have always made me nervous. To me, a healthy sense of fear and nerves make sense.

The [first] time I felt truly comfortable, I was being inducted into the Television Academy Hall of Fame, in 2017. For me success is more about realizing that the race can stop being run, that I could stop worrying that if I slowed down somebody would think my career hadn't worked out or I haven't done a good job.

Over the years I've become interested in what it takes, really, to be a good leader. As I progressed working on my shows, it was important that they not just be run, but run *well*, and in a way that reflected me and my values. But how do you make that happen? In a lot of ways, working on *Scandal* was a huge education because I met professional fixer Judy Smith. *Scandal* was partially inspired by her background in crisis management in Washington, D.C., and learning about her job gave me a lot of keys to leadership. So much so that when I met other interesting, powerful women, I started asking a lot of questions about what they were doing. I asked everybody from Reese Witherspoon, who I think is a smart businesswoman, to Anita Hill, who I think knows the world. Every person you meet has some sort of a gift that you can learn from. The idea that you can't learn something from somebody is always a mistake and an opportunity lost.

One of the biggest things I learned was the idea that everything really does stop and start with you. I saw the difference between passively being good at my piece of my job and working hard to be a leader of my company. You have to be comfortable with the idea that mistakes, no matter what they are, are yours. If the successes are going to be yours, the mistakes are going to be yours too. Because of this, the people who work for you need to be a reflection of your values. Part of being a great leader is hiring amazing people and delegating well, so you can let these great people do the things they are great at, while you do the things *you* are great at. I look to hire people who are passionate about what they do as well as people who will argue with me. I respect that more than anything. A lot of people are willing to tell you exactly what you want to hear at all times, and the sound of your own voice echoing back at you is a very hollow sound. I don't always have the best idea, but somebody else might.

There's real power in admitting you've done something wrong and reapproaching the problem with a solution. The biggest mistake people make in terms of owning power is not being able to admit they don't know something. I watch it happen all the time. Instead of saying, "I don't know that. Can we find somebody who can teach me or tell me more?" people try to hide and pretend. That silence becomes a self-fulfilling prophecy—when you pretend you know something, everybody realizes you don't know anything and lose respect for you. The ability to admit you were wrong or didn't know something is real power and growth.

I never thought there was a problem with being called bossy, bitchy, or difficult. That might be the way I was raised. I was the youngest of six, with a lot of sisters. It just never occurred to me "bossy" was a negative thing. Speaking my mind, standing up for what I want...I was raised to believe I belong in every single room I've ever been in. To be concerned that somebody else thinks I'm bossy or difficult suggests their opinion of me is more important than my own belief in myself.

I wish I'd known two things before I started my career: First, nobody knows what they're doing. There's a feeling when you're younger that certain people really have it together. The thing I find fascinating is that I feel the same way at 50 as I did at 22 and 15, in a lot of ways. I may be more mature, but it's not like you have a wild change in spirit and become this phoenix. Second, I wish I had known everything would be okay. The universe unfolds. I would have enjoyed the moments more as they were happening versus worrying about what was going to come next.

We've all been in a place where we've felt stuck or worried about the future. I was there before I decided to go to film school and before I sold my first script. You have a responsibility to listen to your inner voice telling you something's not working, but that's not an excuse to quit. It's an excuse to pivot. If the thing you're doing isn't working, do something else. Remember, success does not happen immediately. *Grey's Anatomy* was my first television show, but there is no such thing as an overnight success. Stop feeling like a failure if it doesn't happen as fast as you think it should, because *Grey's* came after seven years of me in this town having to sell CDs to buy gas. When I was younger, my friends and I used to say to each other, "You're never going to be as willing to be as poor as you are right now." No matter who you are, where you are, what age you are, you're always going to have more expenses and responsibilities, so you might as well do it now. Take the risk.

Eleven of the world's 18 women leaders in 2010. Top row, from left: Prime Minister Jadranka Kosor, Croatia; Prime Minister Iveta Radičová, Slovakia; Prime Minister Sheikh Hasina, Bangladesh. Middle row: Prime Minister Kamla Persad-Bissessar, Trinidad and Tobago; President Tarja Halonen, Finland; President Laura Chinchilla, Costa Rica; President Ellen Johnson Sirleaf, Liberia; Chancellor Angela Merkel, Germany. Bottom row: President Roza Otunbayeva, Kyrgyzstan; President Dalia Grybauskaitė, Lithuania; Prime Minister Jóhanna Sigurðardóttir, Iceland.

Women Heads of State

WOMEN OF THE YEAR 2010

When Beyoncé asked, "Who run the world? Girls!" she could have quite literally been singing about 2010, a year in which a landmark 18 women served as heads of government—a number that had nearly doubled since 1990. These women did more than break glass ceilings: They changed the world for all people, regardless of gender.

They were: President Laura Chinchilla, Costa Rica; President Cristina Fernández de Kirchner, Argentina; Prime Minister Julia Gillard, Australia; President Dalia Grybauskaitė, Lithuania; President Tarja Halonen, Finland; Prime Minister Sheikh Hasina, Bangladesh; President Ellen Johnson Sirleaf, Liberia; Prime Minister Mari Johanna Kiviniemi, Finland; Prime Minister Jadranka Kosor, Croatia; President Borjana Krišto, Bosnia and Herzegovina; President Doris Leuthard, Switzerland; President Mary McAleese, Ireland; Chancellor Angela Merkel, Germany; President Roza Otunbayeva, Kyrgyzstan; President Pratibha Patil, India; Prime Minister Kamla Persad-Bissessar, Trinidad and Tobago; Prime Minister Iveta Radičová, Slovakia; Prime Minister Jóhanna Sigurðardóttir, Iceland.

By holding some of the highest ranks in the world, they served as an inspiration to younger generations of women, compelling *Glamour* to honor them. "In some countries we have had the right to vote for less than 100 years, so the entry of women into political leadership has caused a tsunami," Radičová, at the time the prime minister of the Slovak Republic, told *Glamour*. Out of the upheaval came some new approaches to governance. "As a woman, my style defines my leadership. It's a gentler, more compassionate approach," Persad-Bissessar, the prime minister of Trinidad and Tobago, explained. "I consult, I listen, and I compromise where it's in the best interest of the citizens."

Bishop Vashti
Murphy McKenzie
spent the first four
years of her role in
Africa overseeing a
region that included
Mozambique,
Lesotho, Swaziland,
and Botswana.

Bishop Vashti Murphy McKenzie

WOMAN OF THE YEAR 2000

In July 2000 more than 10,000 members of the African Methodist Episcopal Church (AME) packed into the Cincinnati Convention Center to elect Vashti Murphy McKenzie, then a 53-year-old mother of three, to the church's 19-person governing body. It was a milestone moment: For the first time in the AME's 213-year history, a woman would hold the highest office.

"All too often we are faced with barriers in every walk of life," McKenzie told *Glamour* later that year. "But this election says: Yes, if it's possible for her, it's possible for me."

In McKenzie the AME now had a powerful, motivating new leader who had built her career on hands-on community activism—or "ministry of empowerment," as she called it. As head of Payne Memorial AME Church in Baltimore, she won a $1.5 million state contract to open a job-training center, more than tripled the church's membership, and created a partnership with a bank to improve resources for her community.

"Now, since the stained-glass ceiling has been broken, don't you dare pick up the pieces and put it back," she said in her Woman of the Year acceptance speech. "If you do you'll have a fight on your hands." McKenzie continued to rise within the leadership ranks at AME, wrote several books on professional growth for women, and served on President Barack Obama's advisory council on faith-based and neighborhood partnerships—forever ensuring the "stained-glass ceiling" would stay broken.

Elizabeth Dole

WOMAN OF THE YEAR 1993 AND 1999

When Elizabeth Dole ran for the Oval Office, in 1999, she knew her presidential bid was a longshot but hoped, at the very least, that she'd inspire more women to get into politics. At that point Dole had devoted 30-plus years to her career, which spanned presidential administrations, two cabinet posts, and a period running the American Red Cross (for which *Glamour* honored her as a Woman of the Year in 1993). Her foundation, the Elizabeth Dole Foundation, created in 2012 and still active in 2020, has empowered and supported the caregivers and families who care for wounded or ill military veterans. Throughout all this, one of her biggest objectives has been equal rights for women.

At *Glamour*'s Women of the Year Awards, she told the audience about a day on the campaign trail when a young girl, about 11 years old, stood up during a question-and-answer period and asked, "Mrs. Dole, if you win this election will your face go up on Mount Rushmore?"

"You know something?" Dole replied. "I think we'd have a good shot at that."

Dole wasn't just inspiring adult women to get into politics. She was inspiring young girls to reach for the highest levels of American government. "I believe that somewhere between the cornfields of Iowa and the covered bridges of New Hampshire, somewhere across America, I shook the hand of a girl who will become president of the United States of America," Dole said in her 1999 WOTY acceptance speech. "And I believe that as she was shaking my hand, she realized, Yes, it can happen."

Tory Burch

WOMAN OF THE YEAR 2011 AND 2019

Tory Burch has always been ambitious. But the designer and businesswoman didn't consider what that word really meant until a male *New York Times* reporter asked her if she was, in 2005. "It was meant to be snarky," she told *Glamour* in her 2019 Woman of the Year profile. "Back then ambition, when it was associated with a woman, was not a positive. And I've been determined to change that harmful stereotype, the one that I bought into myself."

Plus it takes more than just ambition to create an empire. When the former fashion executive opened her first retail store, in 2004, most of the inventory sold out on the first day. Burch made this early success last, though, by constantly evolving the brand. She jumped on ecommerce before it was considered a vital business investment, for example. In 2020 the label had stores in 35 countries around the world.

But Burch's real ambition wasn't in making Forbes Most Powerful lists or opening retail stores. "My plan was always to start a *global* lifestyle brand so that I could start a foundation," she said, which she did in 2009. "People thought it was crazy. I was told never to say 'business' and 'social responsibility' in the same sentence." When the magazine honored her in 2011, the Tory Burch Foundation had partnered with nonprofit Accion to offer small-business loans to women-owned companies. By 2019, when she was honored again, Bank of America was doubling its commitment and offering $100 million in affordable loans.

That investment in women was what made Burch a two-time WOTY honoree. "I've never necessarily wanted to be the biggest company," Burch said. "I wanted to be, obviously, the most profitable—but also the most inspiring place to work." See: ambition.

what it takes TO BECOME A CHAMPION

The women athletes Glamour has honored over the past three decades are champions and pioneers in every sense of the word. They've broken records, won countless medals, and surpassed their rivals—and they are fierce fighters for causes they believe in. Here, in their own words, they share what empowers them. Take note.

TRUST IN YOUR ABILITIES.

"The most important belief is self-belief and self-love. If you have that, you can achieve anything you set out to do."

—SERENA WILLIAMS, TENNIS PLAYER AND 2009 WOMAN OF THE YEAR

EMBRACE FAILURE.

"I'd rather regret the risk that didn't work out than the chances I didn't take at all."

—SIMONE BILES, GYMNAST AND 2016 WOMAN OF THE YEAR

MANIFEST YOUR VICTORY.

"Before the [Women's British Open in 2007] I stood on the 18th green and I knew it was my trophy. Then I enjoyed playing and just let it happen."

—LORENA OCHOA, FORMER GOLFER AND 2007 WOMAN OF THE YEAR

CHOOSE YOUR OWN ADVENTURE.

"No matter what road or path you choose, you have to make some part of it your own. You have to know who you are and own your choices and actions."

—ABBY WAMBACH, FORMER SOCCER PLAYER AND 2015 WOMAN OF THE YEAR

NEVER GIVE UP.

"For all you girls who are striving for your dreams, don't ever stop. Always keep pushing. Don't let anyone or anything stop you."

—GABBY DOUGLAS, GYMNAST AND 2012 WOMAN OF THE YEAR

LOOK TO OTHERS FOR MOTIVATION.

"When I'm defeated, when I'm worn out, and when I ask myself the question, 'Why do I continue to torture my body like this?'... it's phenomenal women [like the Women of the Year] who I continue to turn to for hope and inspiration."

—ALLYSON FELIX, TRACK AND FIELD SPRINTER AND 2012 WOMAN OF THE YEAR

THINK BIGGER THAN YOURSELF.

"To me, true champions lift up others."

—BILLIE JEAN KING, FORMER TENNIS PLAYER AND 2006 WOMAN OF THE YEAR

KEEP SETTING NEW, HIGHER GOALS.

"For women today, there are no limits. We play hard, get down and dirty, and kick butt. And we're going to set new and higher standards for the women athletes of the future."

—LINDSEY VONN, FORMER SKIER AND 2010 WOMAN OF THE YEAR

ACHIEVE— FOR YOURSELF AND *OTHERS*.

"When my teammates and I stepped onto the field, it wasn't just about us. We also played for all the girls in the stands and all their moms who didn't get the opportunities we did."

—MIA HAMM, FORMER SOCCER PLAYER AND 2010 WOMAN OF THE YEAR

Hillary Clinton

WOMAN OF THE YEAR 1992 AND 2008

When *Glamour* honored Hillary Clinton in 1992, the magazine praised her as the White House's "first partner"—as much a power player in American politics and public policy as the recently elected president, Bill, to whom she was married. (Case in point: Clinton was the first first lady to have her own office in the West Wing.) Not since Eleanor Roosevelt had the country seen a first lady so empowered to create change. That was especially visible on September 5, 1995, when Clinton delivered a rousing speech in Beijing in which she proudly declared, "Women's rights are human rights." (Amazingly, that was seen as tremendously radical at the time.)

Clinton then used her platform and experience from the White House to run for public office herself—first as a United States senator, a position she won in 2000, followed by a presidential bid in 2008. Though she lost that race to Barack Obama, himself a history-making candidate as the first Black president, it was the closest a woman had come to the office. For this, *Glamour* honored her with her second Woman of the Year Award. "I was privileged to run for president," she said in her acceptance speech. "Someone asked me the other day, 'If you even knew how it was going to turn out, would you do it all over again?' And I said, 'Absolutely.' Because there are so many ways each and every one of us can make a difference."

When Clinton ran for president again, in 2016, after serving as secretary of state, she made it even further: She was the first woman to be nominated for president by a major U.S. political party. It was a victory for women made all the more devastating when she lost the election. Clinton pledged not to run again, but when a woman does get elected president, she will owe her a tremendous debt. And so will we.

Dolores Huerta

WOMAN OF THE YEAR 2020

Activism is in Dolores Huerta's blood. Born in the mountains of northern New Mexico in 1930, the groundbreaking labor leader and civil rights activist grew up watching her parents fight in their own ways against racial and economic injustice. Her father, a farmworker and miner, was a union activist who served in the state legislature; her mother was a community leader and businesswoman who ran a 70-room hotel and often waived the fee for low-wage workers so they could have shelter.

These traits—compassion for others, the drive to create change—led Huerta to her calling as a trailblazing organizer and political leader. By age 25 she was setting up voter registration drives and pushing for advancements for the local barrio in Stockton, California. Through this work she met labor leader César E. Chávez, who

shared Huerta's goal to improve the lives and wages of agricultural workers. Together, in 1962, they launched the National Farm Workers Association, which later became the United Farm Workers of America. Within a year Huerta had helped secure state-backed aid for dependent families as well as disability insurance for farmworkers in California. A massive grassroots campaign she organized that called for a nationwide grape boycott inspired an estimated 17 million people to stop buying the fruit. It led to the Agricultural Labor Relations Act of 1975, a landmark statute that granted farmworkers the right to organize.

During this time Huerta was also a key figure in the burgeoning feminist movement, where she shared a vision of intersectionality in activism with feminist leader Gloria Steinem—something that

remained an important part of both activists' work. "You know women are always on the front lines," Huerta said. "Women are always doing all of the work. But where somehow women get left behind is when it gets to the decision-making."

Huerta's gift for organizing communities is perhaps best felt in the phrase she coined, "Sí, se puede." Spanish for "Yes, we can," it became a rallying cry for the immigrant rights movement and was co-opted by President Barack Obama for his historic 2008 campaign. When Obama awarded Huerta the Presidential Medal of Freedom in 2012, he said jokingly, "Dolores was very gracious when I told her I had stolen her slogan…. Knowing her, I'm pleased she let me off easy."

In 2020, nine decades into her life, Huerta remains tireless in her work. Arrested nearly two dozen times for protesting—including in 2019 when the then 89-year-old was demonstrating for fair pay for California caretakers—Huerta has continued to advocate for economic, racial, and gender equality. Through her Dolores Huerta Foundation, she also planted the seed for future generations of leaders by helping others run for political office.

"I call it magic dust," Huerta told *Glamour*. "You come into a community and sprinkle magic dust on people and say, 'Look, you can do this. You have the power to make these changes.' Once they understand that, it's just amazing."

"I call myself a born-again feminist," Dolores Huerta said. "Because after working with men for so many decades, at some point I said, 'Hey, wait a minute. There's something wrong here.'"

Chris Evert

WOMAN OF THE YEAR 1990

In 1971 Chris Evert was only 16 years old but already on an impressive winning streak at her first Grand Slam tournament. Evert was new to the tennis scene, but she defeated seasoned pro after seasoned pro to become the youngest semifinalist in U.S. Open history. But when she came up against the legendary Billie Jean King, Evert lost the match. Even so, King recalled, "I went over and told everyone I had just seen the next great champion."

King's prediction proved to be true: For seven years Evert was ranked the number one player in the world. (In nearly two decades of tour, she never ranked lower than number four.) Evert won 18 Grand Slam singles championships and became the first woman to reach $1 million in career prize money.

Evert retired in 1989, and *Glamour* honored her a year later in the magazine's first-ever Women of the Year Awards—not just for the athlete's generation-altering tennis accomplishments but for her immediate career pivot to philanthropy. The same year she retired, she started Chris Evert Charities to help at-risk families in her home state of Florida; through events like pro-celebrity tennis matches, the nonprofit raised more than $26 million in 30 years. Like so many WOTY honorees after her, Evert's accomplishments continued long after she accepted her award. "Helping people is a priority for me," Evert said. "I really feel like I can give back to society because I feel like I've taken so much as it is."

Anne Sweeney

WOMAN OF THE YEAR 2005

Anne Sweeney—"the most powerful woman in entertainment," according to the *Hollywood Reporter*—was not afraid of a comeback challenge. When she took over as president of Disney-ABC Television Group, in 2004, the network was lagging behind in both ratings and cool factor. (The only ABC show in the top 10? *Monday Night Football*.) In just a year under her tenure, ABC was in the top three. More important, she changed the television landscape for women for good: While she was president, ABC developed groundbreaking series like *Grey's Anatomy* and *Desperate Housewives*, forever proving that shows with dynamic women front and center can be ratings gold.

Her famed "sane, ego-free management" style, as *Glamour* praised in 2005, also helped in her success. "I feel very comfortable in the world of [asking], 'What do *you* think?'" she explained in her profile interview. That willingness to collaborate and listen to ideas made her open to forward-thinking technology—like, for example, when she led ABC-Disney to become one of the first studios to put content on Netflix. (A prescient move: Sweeney was named a director on the streaming service's board in 2015, a role she still holds as of July 2020.)

But perhaps the most inspirational aspect of Sweeney was her willingness to challenge not just the networks she runs but also herself. In 2014 she shocked Hollywood when she announced that, at age 56, she was stepping down from ABC-Disney to focus on becoming a television director. Such a career shift was unprecedented in the industry, but Sweeney welcomed the new creative pursuit. "Do the things that scare you the most," she said in her announcement. That passion and adaptability are what made her a *Glamour* Woman of the Year.

Anne Sweeney's management tip? "I feel very comfortable in the world of [asking], 'What do *you* think?'"

Peggy Whitson

WOMAN OF THE YEAR 2017

In July 2020, NASA had 16 active women astronauts eligible for flight assignment—a progressive number considering only 65 women, out of 576 total space travelers, had flown into space since the Soviet Union's Valentina Tereshkova was the first, in 1963. One of those trailblazers is Peggy Whitson, who holds the record for most spacewalks by a woman (10).

"If at first you don't succeed, try, try again" is something astronaut Whitson knows all too well. When Whitson landed a position at NASA as a research associate in 1986, she immediately applied for the astronaut program…and was rejected. Ten years and five attempts later, she was finally approved to start training. But her first liftoff, on the shuttle *Endeavour*, wasn't until 2002. In the years that followed, Whitson broke through several glass ceilings: most spacewalks by a woman astronaut, first woman chief of NASA's astronaut office, and first woman to command the International Space Station among them.

"For me the biggest part of my success has been not being afraid of working hard," Whitson told *Glamour* when she was honored as a Woman of the Year in 2017. At the time she had just broken a new record: 665 days in space—more than any other American astronaut. "There's a quote I've always remembered: You're never given a wish without the power of being able to make it come true. You might have to work for it, however." Roger that.

Laverne Cox

WOMAN OF THE YEAR 2014

When Laverne Cox heard she got the role of inmate Sophia Burset in Netflix's *Orange Is the New Black*, a groundbreaking series about the lives of the women in a federal prison, she dropped everything she was doing to celebrate. This was more than a career breakthrough—it was finally a chance to see a nuanced transgender character on-screen. "I played hookers a lot," Cox said. "That was the scope of what was available for trans actors." She had waited her whole career—her whole life, really—to see something like *Orange Is the New Black* come along. "I need to kill it," she told herself.

And she did: The year Cox was honored as a WOTY, the actor was nominated for an Emmy Award, scored dozens of major magazine covers, and was using her newfound platform as a vocal leader fighting for transgender rights. "I always knew when I got a public platform, it was part of my job to educate people," Cox told *Glamour*. "Being famous to just wear lovely clothes—which I do love doing—that's not for me."

What *is* for her are the connections she made through her work. "I meet people who say that my role has given them the courage to say, 'This is who I am,' and, 'I can transition and be successful and be out as a trans person," she said. "We have this internal compass of the truth inside of us. And that is our job, really—to quiet all this noise around us and listen to that."

"The issues of transgender women are *women's* issues," Laverne Cox said as she accepted her 2014 Woman of the Year Award.

"There are
everythin
is to listen a
to learn
we get b

lessons in
g. Our job
nd continue
so that
etter at life."

—LAVERNE COX, WOMAN OF THE YEAR 2014

Evelyn Lauder

WOMAN OF THE YEAR 1999

As the senior corporate vice president of Estée Lauder Companies, Evelyn Lauder knew beauty. When she joined the cosmetics giant in 1959, the company founded by her in-laws sold only five products (a lipstick, cream, lotion, fragrance, and bath oil); by 1999, when she was honored as a Woman of the Year, it was a $3.6 billion business. But her real impact was in breast cancer awareness: In the early '90s, inspired by the work AIDS activists were doing, Lauder created the pink-ribbon campaign and started the Breast Cancer Research Foundation (BCRF).

"I figured I was good at selling makeup," she told *Glamour* in 1999. "I should be good at selling this cause." She was: When *Glamour* honored Lauder that year, BCRF had in six years raised $18 million for breast cancer research. When we checked in with her almost a decade later, in 2008, Lauder and her team had raised $39.6 million that year alone.

"Anyone can change the world, with vision, even if you start small," she said. "We began with a borrowed office that three people shared. You mustn't get discouraged. If you really believe in it, it will happen."

Lauder died in 2011 from nongenetic ovarian cancer, but the work she started continued: The foundation that she cofounded has been the largest private funder of breast cancer research in the world. Because of her a cure for breast cancer is possible.

How do you change the world? "Anyone can, with vision, even if you start small," Evelyn Lauder told *Glamour* in 2008. "We began with a borrowed office that three people shared. You mustn't get discouraged. If you really believe in it, it will happen."

Christine Lagarde

WOMAN OF THE YEAR 2016

Christine Lagarde grew up with three brothers in Le Havre, France, but she was always the one in charge: According to Lagarde, her eldest sibling learned judo just to keep up with her. Her attitude wasn't any different in the finance world, where Lagarde racked up a number of glass-ceiling-shattering moments as France's first woman finance minister and the first woman managing director of the International Monetary Fund (IMF) in its 70-year history.

Her mission in all of these roles? Prove to world finance leaders that gender equality is good for business, period. "It's not just a fundamentally moral cause," she said. "It is an absolute economic no-brainer. If governments were to address closing the gender gap, if they were to remove the discriminations against women, give them access to the labor market and to finance, a big chunk of the inequalities that we have in many countries would actually disappear. Not all of it, but a lot of it."

In 2016, the same year she was honored as a Woman of the Year, the French court found Lagarde guilty of negligence for her role in an arbitration deal for businessman Bernard Tapie. The IMF's 24-member board, however, stood behind her—former U.S. Treasury secretary Larry Summers said she was "the best thing" to happen to the IMF in a long time.

"I am often referred to as a rock star," Lagarde said at the time, "but I don't think that is really meaningful. What I am always very touched by is when young women, and sometimes young girls, turn to me and say they see me as a role model. If I can help them achieve what they want to achieve, then that's meaningful. That's brilliant."

Serena Williams

WOMAN OF THE YEAR 2009

Serena Williams is often called the Greatest of All Time, but that still doesn't feel like enough when it comes to the tennis player's legacy. "My goal is not to be the best athlete in the world," Williams insisted. "My goal is to help others." That was evident in 2009 when she was named a *Glamour* Woman of the Year.

Alongside her colossal tennis achievements—in 2020 she had more Grand Slam titles, 23 and counting, than any professional still playing, as well as four Olympic medals—her nonprofit, then called the Serena Williams Foundation, had recently opened a school in rural Kenya. "When I cut the ribbon at that school, I felt so genuinely happy," Williams told *Glamour*. "I've never felt that way winning Wimbledon or any other tournament. And I have won them *all*."

In the decade-plus following her Woman of the Year win, she continued to dominate on and off the court. She overcame injuries, built on the success of her namesake fashion line, launched her venture firm Serena Ventures, forced the Women's Tennis Association to reform its maternity leave practices after speaking about being unfairly penalized upon her return from maternity leave (following the birth of her daughter, Alexis Olympia Ohanian Jr., in 2017, with husband Alexis Ohanian), raised awareness of the disturbing number of Black maternal mortality rates, and tackled racism and sexism in the game.

"When most people would falter, she is able to raise her game a level, and that's what you look for in champions," Billie Jean King, a tennis champion and 2006 Woman of the Year, told *Glamour*.

"I try to be the best that I can be every day," Williams explained in a 2016 *Glamour* interview. "I have bad days. I had a bad day the other day. I hit for only, like, 30 minutes, and I stormed off the court. But that was the best I could do on that day. So am I the greatest? I don't know. I'm the greatest that *I* can be."

"I use the trophies as punch bowls," Serena Williams said jokingly to *Glamour* in 2009.

"It's all happening now," Vanessa Williams said as she accepted her 1994 Woman of the Year Award. "I'm having a wonderful year... and I think that my best years are yet to come."

Vanessa Williams

WOMAN OF THE YEAR 1994

In 1983 Vanessa Williams made history as the first Black woman to be crowned Miss America since the competition was founded in 1921—only to be forced to resign 10 months later after unauthorized nude photographs of her were published in *Penthouse*. But by the time *Glamour* honored Williams a decade later, she had overcome that obstacle (and then some) to become, as the magazine praised, "the first Miss America in decades to achieve a renown beyond the pageant."

Williams had learned a valuable lesson from her time in, and out of, the spotlight: Be adaptable. "I'm always learning," she told *Glamour*. "I'm always trying. I'm always failing. I'm always coping. Nothing is permanent. You've got to go with the flow and do the best that you can."

That knowledge didn't come easy. After Williams resigned her Miss America title, many thought her career was over before it had even really begun. Not Williams. She had won the talent portion of Miss America by singing, so she parlayed that into a record contract. Her first three singles were all hits, earning her multiple Grammy nominations. From that success Williams booked a full lineup of hit TV shows and movies, as well as multiple successful stints on Broadway.

"I dared to have a dream when people thought I deserved naught," she said, crediting her parents for giving her a loving environment that empowered her to fight. "My parents told me I could do whatever I wanted to do. Having that mantra growing up has made me into the successful woman that I am. I'm trying to instill that into my own kids."

Mary Robinson

WOMAN OF THE YEAR 2005

"As the only girl wedged between four brothers, I had an early interest in human rights," Mary Robinson told *Glamour* in 2005. She may have been laughing when she said it, but it wasn't a joke: The first woman president of Ireland, elected in 1990, Robinson made sweeping changes that set an example for *all* leaders worldwide. Among her progressive platforms, the politician used her time as president to legalize birth control, reform rape laws, and push for LGBTQ+ rights.

"She is endlessly committed to the principle that every individual counts," said former secretary of state Madeleine Albright.

This work continued long after Robinson left office in 1997. When *Glamour* honored her in 2005, she had recently left a role as the United Nations High Commissioner for Human Rights and was working on her organization Realizing Rights, a global initiative committed to enhancing greater equality for all. Her goal, she said at the time, was to create more equal-opportunity leadership. "Not for the sake of women," she explained. "For the sake of all humanity."

Elected in 1990, Mary Robinson was the first woman president of Ireland.

Heads of the Class

WOMEN OF THE YEAR 2007

Fact: More women graduate from college than men. Associate's, bachelor's, master's, or doctorate—whatever the level of education, women have been out there surpassing men in all categories since the beginning of the 21st century. And yet the "joke" that women seeking higher education just want an M.R.S. degree (read: married) has persisted since Catherine Brewer, the first American woman to get a bachelor's, graduated in 1840.

But in 2007 that collegiate boys'-club mentality got a shake-up when Drew Gilpin Faust, Ph.D., became the first woman president of Harvard University. Her appointment was a milestone in academia: For the first time ever, half of the Ivy League schools were helmed by women. Faust joined Amy Gutmann, Ph.D., president of the University of Pennsylvania; Ruth Simmons, Ph.D., president of Brown University; and Shirley Tilghman, Ph.D., president of Princeton University in leading four of the most prestigious schools in the country.

"If I had to think about why *Glamour* chose the four of us to honor this year,

I hope it is because they believe, as we do, in the enormous power of education to truly transform lives and to empower women," Tilghman said as she accepted the award that year. "I come, as do my friends, from a generation where women were told that a college education would be wasted on them. That their role was to become married and raise families, and an education would be simply superfluous.... Darwin famously said it is neither the strong nor the most intelligent who ultimately prevail. It is those who are most able to adapt to change. And what I would say of Harvard, Brown, the University of Pennsylvania, and Princeton University is that those great, venerable, tradition-bound institutions not only adapted to change but they have led change."

And they have changed the universities for the better. By encouraging women scholars to pursue careers in male-dominated fields, they have made a lasting impact that we'll see for generations to come.

From left, in 2007: Drew Gilpin Faust, president of Harvard University; Amy Gutmann, president of the University of Pennsylvania; Ruth Simmons, president of Brown University; and Shirley Tilghman, president of Princeton University.

Arianna Huffington

WOMAN OF THE YEAR 2011

"I feel so profoundly that each one of us has a unique destiny," Arianna Huffington said. *Her* destiny? Mastering the art of the career pivot, trading one successful venture for the next. The self-proclaimed "Greek peasant girl" has been a popular political commentator (first as a Republican, then a Democrat), once ran for governor of California, and is a *New York Times* best-selling author.

Her most risky—and profitable—venture was her 2005 launch of the *Huffington Post*. At the time websites featuring news, gossip, and first-person narratives all in one place were unheard of, and critics were quick to share their skepticism. Huffington pushed on. "People underestimate how truly brilliant she is," her friend Nora Ephron said. "She is an unstoppable comet." By 2011, when she was a *Glamour* Woman of the Year, the site had more than 225 million visitors worldwide. She sold the *Huffington Post* to AOL for $315 million, and in 2016 she was on to her next endeavor, stepping down from her role as editor in chief to launch Thrive Global, a platform focused on providing science-based solutions to stress and burnout.

To be successful, Huffington has proven, you must take risks. "If my daughters, and women of all ages, are to take their rightful place in society, they must become fearless," Huffington said. "If you want to succeed big, there is no substitute for simply sticking your neck out."

"ONWARD, UPWARD, AND INWARD!"

Arianna Huffington started Thrive Global in 2016 with a lofty but important mission: to use science and fact-based research to change the way people work and live. Here she shares how her own stress and burnout led to a pioneering new business model.

MY MOTHER DIDN'T GO TO COLLEGE. She never had a job or any direct reports, unless you count me and my sister, Agapi. And yet, long before I entered the world of work, she taught me what it means to be a leader.

Of course, I didn't know it was happening at the time. In our one-bedroom apartment in Athens, my mother would preside over long sessions in our small kitchen, dis-

cussing the principles and teachings of Greek philosophy to help guide me and Agapi in our decisions and our choices. She was the one who taught me about a different definition of success and the need to do everything we can to protect and nurture our human capital, because building and looking after our financial capital is not enough. And she taught me that failure is not the opposite of success; she used to say,

"Failure is a stepping stone to success."

My mother was also the catalyst for my first real leadership role, as president of Cambridge Union debate society. I was 14 years old when I saw a photo of Cambridge in a magazine, and I was desperate to go there. Everyone told me that this was ridiculous—I spoke no English, we had no money, and it was hard even for English girls to get into Cambridge. My mother was the only person who said: Let's see how we can make it happen. And so I learned English, took my GCEs through the British Consul, applied for a scholarship, and ended up studying economics at Cambridge.

At 21, I was elected president of the debating society, which led to my getting an offer to write my first book on the changing role of women—a topic of one of the debates I had participated in. After my first book was published and then the second and third, and through the launch of the *Huffington Post* and Thrive Global, I began to see the value of something else my mother had taught me. By word and by deed, she regularly demonstrated the value of having a support group of family and friends—what I now call my "Thrive tribe"—in place to give you honest feedback, to support you when the going gets tough, to help salve your wounds, and, just as important, to help you celebrate and appreciate the good times too.

This is especially important for working women, who still face an ingrained double standard wherein the same behaviors that help men get ahead and prove their worth on the job are often discouraged in women.

As working women we have to weigh the psychic cost of not trying a new job or venture against the possibility of not succeeding and being embarrassed by our efforts. The former creates regret, the latter a few hours—or perhaps a few days—of licking our wounds. I've learned again and again in my career that if you want to succeed, there is no substitute for simply sticking your neck out and being willing to risk failure.

And the world desperately needs women willing to do that. Especially now, when leadership qualities traditionally identified with women—empathy, collaboration, team building—are more important than ever.

In my role as *HuffPost*'s editor in chief, I experienced one of my biggest leadership failures. Two years in we were growing at an incredible pace. I was on the cover of magazines and had been chosen by *Time* as one of the world's 100 Most Influential People. But on the morning of April 6, 2007, I was lying on the floor of my home office in a pool of blood. On my way down, my head had hit the corner of my desk, cutting my eye and breaking my cheekbone. I had collapsed from exhaustion and lack of sleep. After my fall I had to ask myself, Was this what success looked like? Was this the life I wanted? I was working 18 hours a day, seven days a week, trying to build a business, expand our coverage, and bring in investors. But my life, I realized, was out of control. In terms of the traditional measures of success, which focus on money and status, I was very successful. But I was not living a successful life by any sane definition of success. I knew something had to change radically. I could not go on that way.

That painful wake-up call informed everything that followed, including the founding of Thrive Global in 2016. Thrive's mission is to end the stress and burnout epidemic—a mission that, not coincidentally, is directly connected to the kind of leadership we need in the 21st century. And women are in a unique position to change the culture of leadership. Because for far too long men have equated success with working around the clock, driving yourself into the ground, sleep deprivation, and burnout.

The leaders we need are those who can shift our entire culture away from an always-on, perpetually stressed-out, fight-or-flight state of being and reconnect with some essential truths we have forgotten. Because while the world provides plenty of insistent, flashing, high-volume signals directing us to make more money and climb higher up the ladder, there are almost no worldly signals reminding us to stay connected to the essence of who we are, to take care of ourselves along the way, to reach out to others, to pause to wonder, and to connect to that place from which everything is possible.

We cannot become the leaders we need by playing by the same rules that have led us into so many crises. We need a new leadership playbook. This begins with putting our own oxygen mask on first. When we take care of ourselves, we see benefits to our physical and mental health, performance, and productivity. When we don't, we pay a price: innovation, creativity, resilience, empathy, decision-making, and team building are the first to disappear when we are burned out and depleted.

In times of deep uncertainty like these, in order for leaders to be able to see the icebergs ahead and recognize the hidden opportunities, they need to find a way to get themselves into the metaphorical eye of the hurricane—that centered place of strength, wisdom, and peace that we all have inside ourselves. This was the place that Marcus Aurelius, the emperor of Rome for 19 years—facing plagues, invasions, and betrayals—described in his book *Meditations* (the only leadership book I have by my nightstand!). Because only from that place can we come up with our most innovative and creative ideas that the times demand.

If there is one thing I wish I knew earlier in my career, it is this: Your performance, decision-making, and ability to lead will actually improve if you can commit to not only working hard but also unplugging, recharging, and renewing yourself.

It's a way of working and living my mother would approve of. And it's one we need to role model every day if we're going to emerge from the challenges of our unprecedented times into a better, fairer, more compassionate world. "Onward, upward, and inward" is how I end many of my speeches. My own experience bears witness to the truth that we cannot thrive and lead the lives we want without learning to go inward. This is a fundamental principle of leadership that we can no longer neglect. So to every woman who aspires to be a leader, I say: Find a way to get yourself into the eye of the hurricane. Find your place of wisdom and peace and strength. And from that place, remake the world in your own image, according to your own definition of success, so that all of us—women and men—can thrive and live our lives with more grace, more joy, more compassion, more gratitude, and yes, more love. Onward, upward, and inward!

Pamela Thomas-Graham

WOMAN OF THE YEAR 2001

A few days after September 11 had traumatized the country, Pamela Thomas-Graham sat down and wrote a letter to her three-year-old son.

At the time Thomas-Graham had just become the CEO of financial news network CNBC and was one of the highest-ranking women at NBC—for which she was being honored as a *Glamour* Woman of the Year. She had a bachelor's degree, a juris doctorate, and an MBA from Harvard and still found time to publish two mystery novels with Simon & Schuster. But for all her world experience, Thomas-Graham had never seen such a collective rise to the occasion as she did after 9/11. "I thought that someday I might want him to look back and read about what his mom was learning about leadership in this extraordinary time of challenge," she said in her speech at the 2001 WOTY Awards.

This is what she told him: "I think there are some new characteristics that leaders need to demonstrate now, and I think they are characteristics that women have always had and continue to show. The first one is endurance.... A leader goes in first and stays until the end and shows that it's alright to get back to business. The second quality is compassion.... It's a quality that traditionally was not expected of business leaders in such copious quantities as it is now, but I think that CEOs who are leading the charge are the ones who are showing compassion. And the third thing is that leaders have to be collaborative. Today, a leader has to show endurance and compassion, to be collaborative, and to do it all with grace and a good sense of humor."

Though Thomas-Graham, who went on to be the group president of Liz Claiborne, wrote that letter in 2001, her advice on leadership in action remains as true as ever. Endurance, compassion, and collaboration—these are traits that all *Glamour*'s Women of the Year honorees, including Thomas-Graham, have shown. Remember them.

In 2001 Pamela Thomas-Graham was running CNBC as CEO, raising a three-year-old, and working on her third murder-mystery novel. "Having so much going on helps keep me focused," she told *Glamour* at the time.

Condoleezza Rice

WOMAN OF THE YEAR 2008

"The most important thing you can do in life," former secretary of state Condoleezza Rice said as she accepted her 2008 Woman of the Year Award, "is to find a passion."

Rice discovered hers as a student at the University of Denver when she attended a class on international politics. Her worldview opened up so much that she was inspired to switch her major from music—she's a classically trained pianist—to political science. "When you find your passion, you'll realize that you didn't find it," she said in her speech. "It found you...and *then* you can go on to try to make a difference in the world on the basis of that passion."

Rice would know a thing or two about trying to make a difference: After an established career in academia and the private sector, as well as stints as a political consultant, she was appointed President George W. Bush's national security advisor, the first woman in history to hold that position, in 2001. Five years later she was promoted to secretary of state, becoming the first Black woman and second-ever woman to hold that position (Madeleine Albright was the first in 1997).

Her tenure was not without controversy: She faced criticism for being a key backer of the Iraq War (2003–2011) and the faulty intelligence that was cited in its favor. But in 2008 *Glamour* honored her as a Woman of the Year for successfully getting the U.N. Security Council to officially recognize rape as a weapon of war—a mission Rice had undertaken after hearing first-hand accounts from women in Darfur who had survived sexual violence. "Rape was always viewed as a circumstance of war, either hush-hush or not in the category of other crimes against humanity," Rice told *Glamour* at the time. "This is a strong message that yes, it is [a crime]."

2001

Editor in Chief **Bonnie Fuller**

1998

I HAD BEEN TO *GLAMOUR*'S WOMEN OF THE YEAR AWARDS before I started as editor in chief in 1998, and I always thought it was fantastic. There weren't a lot of award shows for women with different professions and backgrounds at that time, so I was really impressed. *Glamour* has always been a groundbreaker and a leader in supporting women who are working to fulfill all of their aspirations. I had been a reader ever since I was 12 or 13 years old, and it definitely was an influence on my life. It made me think bigger about my own career.

So I was very excited to be the editor in chief and take over the Women of the Year Awards that Ruth Whitney had established with editor Judith Daniels. I wanted to honor what they had started while also growing the awards in scope and production. My editors and I gave each nominee a tremendous amount of thought because we wanted to recognize women who were groundbreakers and leaders from a variety of backgrounds. I felt very humbled to honor these courageous women, and there were a lot of late nights reading about all of the proposed candidates. It was hard to make decisions because there are so many worthy women in the world who deserved to be celebrated.

In my first year as editor in chief, 1998, we honored Waris Dirie, a model who campaigned against female genital mutilation. I felt it was vital to put a spotlight on the work she was doing, and it was a poignant moment at the awards when she described the physical pain and emotional terror of what she went through. I was proud we could honor her for her courage. I was also inspired

by Pat Summitt, another honoree that year, who was the coach of the University of Tennessee women's basketball team, the Lady Volunteers. She enabled these young women to win eight NCAA Division 1 championships at a time when women's sports was not as well respected as it should have been. She had to fight for support for her team, and she was a dynamic, brilliant woman. In the following years Summitt was awarded the Presidential Medal of Freedom by President Barack Obama, and she also received the Arthur Ashe Courage Award at the 2012 ESPY Awards. My point is that all of these women recognized by *Glamour* continued to grow in their roles long after they were honored as Women of the Year.

That is also true of the women we honored in 1999 and 2000. Jennifer Lopez went on to become even more of a massive force. She started as a dancer and then pursued acting and singing, but she wanted to get into the business side of the entertainment world even back then. I remember her talking about wanting to be a decision maker and a creator, and that's exactly what she did. It's been incredible to watch how she took charge of her career and really owned it. Evelyn Lauder was the most wonderful, warm, and brilliant person, so I was thrilled to honor her for her role in raising millions for more effective and lifesaving treatments for breast cancer. Even though she has passed, her legacy lives on. So many women are alive today because of the money she raised that went toward discovering more effective treatments. The 1999 U.S. Women's National Soccer Team was breaking barriers for young women in sports, and the team continues to win world championships. It's extremely frustrating that in 2020 they were still fighting for the equal pay they deserve. We may have honored them with a parade in New York City to mark their World Cup win in 2019, but they haven't been honored when it comes to their pocketbooks. But they're not going to give up. It just shows how hard it is to make change happen. It makes me realize that as far as we've come, we still have so many fights ahead.

But when I look back at the lineup of women we honored, I see that so many are still leading and creating, and it's encouraging to see the longevity that women can have in their careers. These women aren't just famous for the moment—they are committed for the long haul to their goals and to fulfill all their aspirations. And that is really inspiring.

Ashley Graham

WOMAN OF THE YEAR 2016

"When you're the first of something, you are always going to have to answer the hard questions," Ashley Graham said in a 2018 *Glamour* cover interview. "People are going to be confused by you because you're the new kid in town." While Graham is certainly not the first curvy supermodel, she has reached other milestones in fashion—including being the first size-16 model to appear on the cover of *Sports Illustrated*'s Swimsuit Issue, in 2016. This made her a star, and she wanted to use her platform for good. "If you ask *me*, I'm not the new kid in town," she explained. "This body's been around for centuries, and now I've just been given a voice."

For being such a fierce champion for body positivity, *Glamour* honored Graham with a WOTY Award that year. To mark the occasion, Mattel even created a Barbie doll in her likeness. While Graham was excited about the opportunity, she had one important request: The doll should have zero thigh-gap. (Mattel and *Glamour* made it happen.)

In everything Graham has achieved since that landmark *SI* cover and her WOTY win—countless appearances on the runway, a stint as a judge on *America's Next Top Model*, a Revlon brand ambassador contract, her own clothing lines— she has continued to push for change and more size-inclusivity in fashion. It wasn't just about revolutionizing the industry, though; it was something far greater. "I hope girls look in the mirror and say, 'I am beautiful,'" she said in her *Glamour* WOTY interview. "When you do that, it's a whole other ball game—you start to understand that your words have power."

"Be your own model, and that the wo you are wom lift up. You their

kind of role
remember
men around
en you can
can change
lives."

—ASHLEY GRAHAM, WOMAN OF THE YEAR 2016

Ann Fudge

WOMAN OF THE YEAR 1995

In 1995, when Ann Fudge—then the executive vice president of Kraft Foods Inc. and president of Maxwell House Coffee Company, a $1.5 billion operation—was honored with a Woman of the Year Award, you could count on one hand the number of women CEOs who had led Fortune 500 companies. "We have to change that," Fudge said in her rousing speech. "And I hope in my lifetime—I expect in my lifetime—that we will see that change."

She did: In 2020 the number of women running Fortune 500 companies reached an all-time high with 37 helming brands such as UPS, Gap Inc., and Rite Aid. Fudge herself eventually earned the chair-CEO title in 2003 when she was tapped to run communications company Young & Rubicam Brands. She was also a key part of former president Barack Obama's administration, serving as a member of his campaign's finance committee in 2008 and the National Commission on Fiscal Responsibility and Reform in 2010.

For Fudge, though, who as of 2020 sat on a number of corporate boards, the real excitement comes when she can turn around a challenging company—something she's accomplished a lot. "When people tell me, 'You can't grow this business,'" she said, "that's when it gets fun."

"I want to live to be 110," Ann Fudge told *Glamour* in 1995. "I'm only just getting started."

Jackie Joyner-Kersee

WOMAN OF THE YEAR 1992

When Jackie Joyner-Kersee was born, in early March 1962, her grandmother had a vision: They should name the baby after President John F. Kennedy's wife, Jacqueline. Because, she said, "Someday this girl will be the first lady of something."

And she was. Joyner-Kersee is widely regarded as the greatest track and field athlete of all time. In 2020 she was the most decorated woman in the sport's history with three gold, one silver, and two bronze Olympic medals, and she still held the world record for most points scored in the demanding seven-event heptathlon after setting it in 1988. The 7,000-point threshold had been reached only 10 times since 1984—and six of those were Joyner-Kersee.

In 1992, the year *Glamour* honored her as a WOTY, she had scored her second gold medal and was already training for the 1996 Olympics, the last of her long career. And she accomplished all this while battling severe asthma—she couldn't even take common prescription drugs to treat it because they were banned in competition as stimulants, and she was hospitalized twice because of the condition.

When Joyner-Kersee retired in 1998, she was ready for her next chapter. Retirement meant she had even more time for her passion: tirelessly advocating for children's education through the Jackie Joyner-Kersee Foundation, helping underprivileged young people in her hometown of East St. Louis, Illinois, pursue their dreams. "Age is no barrier," she said. "It's a limitation you put on your mind."

Jackie Joyner-Kersee is the most decorated woman in track and field history with three gold, one silver, and two bronze Olympic medals.

Sherrilyn Ifill

WOMAN OF THE YEAR 2020

Ever since she was very young, Sherrilyn Ifill wanted to be a civil rights lawyer. Her senior yearbook photo even declared, proudly, "Career Goal: Supreme Court Justice."

Though she hasn't taken a seat on the nation's highest court—yet—Ifill is on her way as the head of the NAACP Legal Defense and Educational Fund, Inc. (LDF), the second woman to lead the organization in its 80-year history.

Ifill has dedicated her career to this pursuit of creating change through law. After starting as a fellow at the American Civil Liberties Union, she joined the LDF in 1988 and spent years there litigating landmark voting rights cases. She left to teach civil procedure and constitutional law at the University of Maryland Francis King Carey School of Law, where she did pioneering work creating one of the nation's first law clinics focused on challenging legal barriers to the reentry of ex-offenders into society. In 2013 she returned to the LDF, where she battles voter suppression, racial discrimination, and racial and economic inequality. "She speaks for all those people out there who are facing challenges, who are disenfranchised," singer-songwriter John Legend told *Glamour*. "She fights for them, and she does it with style, with grace, with empathy, and with the force of her determination and her intelligence."

As president and director-counsel of the LDF, the premier law organization fighting for racial justice in the U.S., Ifill is a pivotal advocate for equality. That was especially crucial in summer 2020 as the country entered a period of social uprising not seen since the civil rights movement of the 1960s. The deaths of George Floyd, Breonna Taylor, and many more Black lives at the hands of white police officers sparked an outpouring of grief and calls to end police brutality, violence, and systemic racism. It was a time of reckoning—and Ifill had the tools necessary to create change.

"The multiracial protests we are seeing in all 50 states is a source of optimism," Ifill told *Glamour* in her Women of the Year profile. "We [at the LDF] help advance this movement when we use our credibility to articulate ideas that some people find frightening."

"It takes an entire ecosystem to make transformational change," she continued. "[Civil rights leader] Charles Sherrod once described racism as a shape-shifter. As civil rights lawyers our job is to be like [the heroes] in the old horror movies—able to see the werewolf in its many guises."

"The only way a real and thriving democracy survives is by embracing and investing in public goods like transportation, education, and health care," Sherrilyn Ifill told *Glamour* in 2020.

Bobbi Brown

WOMAN OF THE YEAR 1997

In the 1980s, when cosmetics were all about bold colors and excess, makeup artist Bobbi Brown wanted something different: moderation. So she consulted a chemist and came up with a line of lipsticks in natural shades. It launched at Bergdorf Goodman in 1991 and was such an immediate hit for its pioneering take on beauty that global brand Estée Lauder bought the company just four years later for a reported $74.5 million.

Brown was able to maintain creative control—a rarity in the business—and used that to ensure her brand stayed true to its mission: There's no such thing as "flaws." She was one of the first to embrace the "no-makeup makeup" look that would later dominate the beauty industry.

"I always tell women to be who you are—this means everything from learning to love your lines to appreciating your unique features," she told *Glamour* in a 2015 interview. "For me, being beautiful isn't just about how you look. The most compelling beauty is self-confidence."

Though Brown eventually stepped down from her namesake company in 2016, she continued to build her empire around fostering beauty inside and out. In 2019 she launched a line of health and beauty supplements, called Evolution_18, with the goal of making the wellness trend more accessible. In a world where encouraging self-acceptance remains a radical act, Brown is a leader.

Barbara Walters

WOMAN OF THE YEAR 1999

Barbara Walters has interviewed everyone from Fidel Castro to Katharine Hepburn, created the pioneering (and highly rated) daytime talk show *The View*, and has been honored with dozens of lifetime achievement awards for her respected work as a broadcast journalist. But it was a long journey to get there: When Walters was a reporter at *The Today Show* in the 1970s, she wasn't even allowed to speak while hosting a joint interview until her male coworker had asked the first three questions.

Walters persisted, eventually becoming the morning program's first woman cohost, but the sexism she faced at *Today* wasn't the last challenge she'd overcome during her career. In 1976 she left *Today* for ABC to become the first woman coanchor of a network news program. The gig didn't last long. "I was a big flop," she said during her 1999 *Glamour* Woman of the Year speech, where she was honored with a lifetime achievement award. "I was working with a partner who didn't want to have a woman [on the show]; the audience really didn't either.... I thought it was the end of my career." Of course, it wasn't. She continued interviewing world leaders up until 2016, and *The View*, which she launched in 1997, continued to draw in more than 3 million viewers a week well into 2020.

The point of her story, Walters explained, is that the challenging moments she overcame—not the career highs or glamorous moments—are what she looks back on most fondly. "That road back," she said, "can very often be the most important road with the greatest reward at the end."

Gabby Giffords

WOMAN OF THE YEAR 2011 AND 2013

"Gabby Giffords is a shining example of strength, perseverance, and the ideals that transcend party or politics," former president Barack Obama told *Glamour* in 2011 about the Arizona congresswoman. "She has devoted her career to the idea of working together to make the lives of her fellow Arizonans—and fellow Americans—better."

In January that year, Giffords was shot point-blank in the head during an event with her constituents outside a Tucson supermarket. Six others were killed by the gunman, and Giffords was left fighting for her life. It took unimaginable strength, along with the heroic efforts of her doctors, therapists, and husband, Mark Kelly, but Giffords recovered. That August the Democratic representative returned to the House floor and was greeted with an emotional standing ovation from members of both parties. "I've never seen a reception like that—bipartisan, prolonged, and heartfelt," House Speaker Nancy Pelosi told *Glamour* at the time.

When *Glamour* honored her with a Woman of the Year Award that November, Giffords was not yet healthy enough to travel, so Kelly, a retired U.S. Navy captain and NASA astronaut (who in 2020 was elected U.S. senator for Arizona), accepted on her behalf. "I know what it takes to be a Woman of the Year," he told the teary-eyed audience. "I see it in her every day."

Two years later, the emotion in the room was even more powerful when Giffords took the stage with Kelly to accept her second Woman of the Year Award. They were both honored for their work creating Americans for Responsible Solutions (ARS), a gun-safety organization determined to install basic measures like background checks to keep firearms out of the wrong hands. Among the 12 women being celebrated that night, Kelly pointed out, three had been greatly affected by gun violence: Giffords; Malala Yousafzai, who had been shot by a Taliban gunman for simply trying to go to school; and Kaitlin Roig-DeBellis, a first-grade teacher at Sandy Hook Elementary School who saved 15 students during a mass shooting.

In the years following her award, Giffords has remained a vocal advocate for stricter gun control. "I'm still fighting to make the world a better place," Giffords said in her 2013 speech. "And you can too."

Gabby Giffords
with her husband,
Mark Kelly, in 2013.

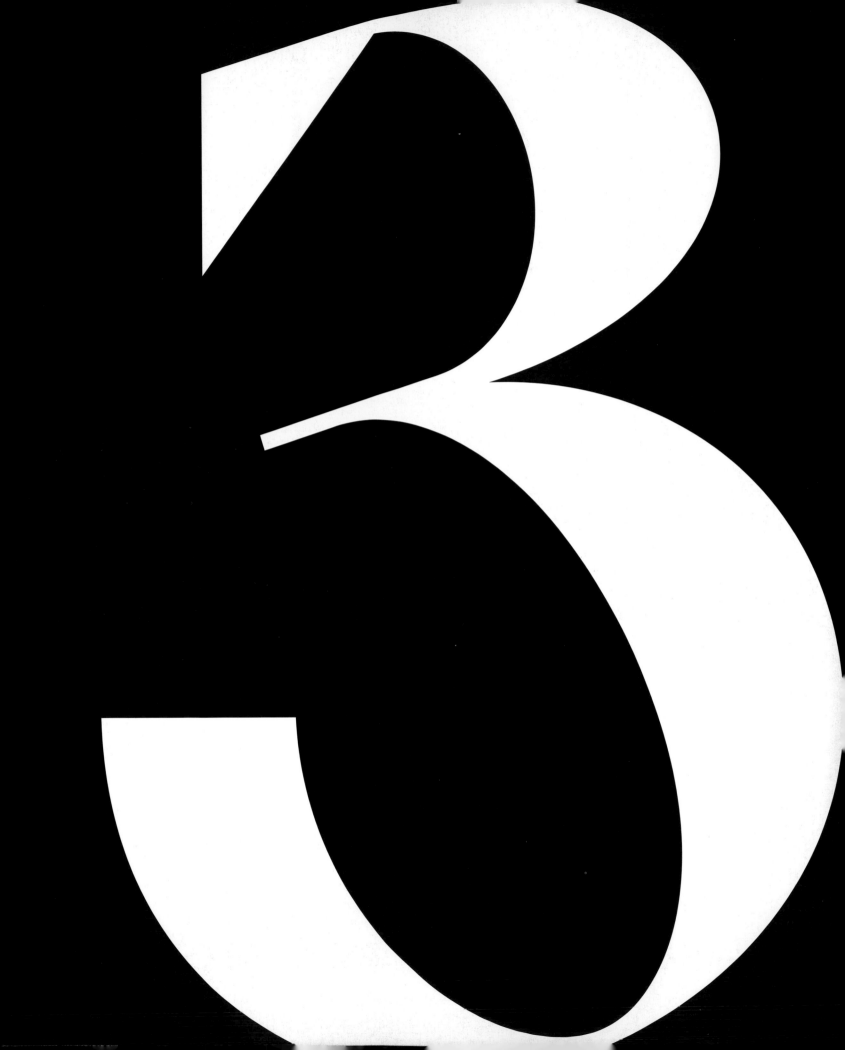

VOICES & VISIONARIES

Whether it's through art or acts of service, these storytellers, creators, and insightful women have used their platforms to push boundaries and enrich our minds.

Michelle Obama

The Obamas had barely been in the White House a year when first lady Michelle Obama was honored with a special-recognition Woman of the Year Award. Her achievements were already seismic—in every action she had undertaken and in everything her position symbolized to millions of Americans. She was, as Katie Couric (who interviewed her for *Glamour*) noted, "the first African American first lady, who, as the great-great-great-granddaughter of a slave, is a powerful symbol of our nation's progress." And, as Couric observed, she was also the rare political player who "still seems so disarmingly, charmingly *normal.*"

Her accomplishments, however, were far from standard. As soon as she moved into the White House, Obama used her new platform and background in law and nonprofit organizations to advocate for everything from education reform to healthy eating. "I think that mentoring is such a critical part of the role I can play in this position," Obama told *Glamour* at the time. "I see how little bits of exposure and big bits of exposure really change my girls significantly, and I want that for more girls around the country and the world."

Obama's passion for empowering others started early, but it grew more focused after she graduated from Harvard Law School and started working in a big law firm. "I thought, There are so many kids like me, in my neighborhood, that could be here [if they had] more support from their families, better financial aid. But the gap is so wide once you miss that opportunity," she said. "So I was always interested in figuring out: How do you bridge that? I felt, as a lawyer, when I was mentoring and working with kids, that I gained a level of groundedness that I just couldn't get sitting on the 47th floor of a fancy firm. Selfishly, it gives me joy—it makes me feel like my life has a purpose. And I thought, Imagine what we can do in the White House, particularly with the kids in the D.C. area, many of whom have never set foot on the White House lawn." She did this through initiatives like her Let's Move! campaign, which invited kids to help plant a new White House garden.

Since leaving the White House in 2017, Obama has remained a source of inspiration for young women around the globe. Her memoir *Becoming,* released in 2018, has sold more than 10 million copies worldwide and served as the basis for a sold-out tour in which Obama held conversations with prominent leaders, including Gayle King and Reese Witherspoon, in front of thousands.

But it is girls' education that continues to propel Obama forward, with the foundation of her Girls Opportunity Alliance in 2018. "My advice to girls is always this—and this is what I tell my daughters every day—do not be afraid to fail," she recalled at a *Glamour* summit in 2016. "Because that oftentimes is the thing that keeps us as women and girls back. The only way you succeed in life, the only way you learn, is by failing. It's not the failure; it's what you do after you fail.

"And the last thing that I do want to say to all girls is: Be supportive of each other…. We cannot compete and see one person's failure as our success. We can all rise together. We can all win."

"There are so many really good role models out there," Michelle Obama said. "We just have to make sure that we don't glorify just one type."

Yara Shahidi

WOMAN OF THE YEAR 2019

When Yara Shahidi, then 19, took the stage at the 2019 *Glamour* Women of the Year Awards, she didn't have a speech prepared. Because, she told the rapt audience, she knew the words would come to her in the moment. Oh, how they did.

That wasn't a surprise to anyone in the room, which included honorees like soccer champion Megan Rapinoe and acclaimed director Ava DuVernay. After all, Shahidi was recognized that year for being a leading voice of Gen Z. The Harvard student and *Grown-ish* actor had already made the Forbes 30 Under 30 list, won NAACP awards, started the voting initiative Eighteen x 18, and interviewed Hillary Clinton. But Shahidi's speech at the WOTY Awards felt especially poetic to those gathered— it was a motivating call to action to do better, be better, and make an impact.

"To be a woman is to understand the power of our yes," she said in her speech, "but to understand how groundbreaking and system-shaking it is to say no. No is productive. Our no doesn't just sit still saying, I am okay being discontent with the system in front of me. Our no takes action. Our no stands up. Our no is allyship. Our no understands that I must advocate for something greater than myself because I am you and you are me and we are of each other."

What remains a through line in everything she does—whether it's activism, acting, or simply a post on Instagram—is that there must be a greater purpose, said Shahidi in her WOTY profile. "That purpose may be as simple as providing joy, or it may be helping in the field of equity or amplifying other people's voices," she said. "But my metric for success is having an impact on something greater than myself."

Toni Morrison

WOMAN OF THE YEAR 2007

When Toni Morrison took the stage to accept her 2007 *Glamour* Woman of the Year lifetime achievement award, a reverent hush fell over the crowd—hard to achieve in a venue as large as New York City's Carnegie Hall, but an appropriate reaction when one of the greatest American novelists is about to speak. "I have borne witness for 60 years to the changes in women's lives, the unapologetic and the unfrenzied rise of women to responsible places in public," Morrison opened. "And I have to say that my own background is humble only in one respect, and that is money. In every other way it was rich in expectations."

Very early in her life, she explained, it was made clear to her that there was no safety net being a Black woman in America. "I was to be willing to step outside the gate that others had constructed for me," she said. "My job was to make sure that whatever gifts I had were not wasted, were not compromised, and were not a cause for protected status."

Wasted they were not. Morrison authored 11 novels, several children's books coauthored with her son Slade, and two plays. Her third novel, *Song of Solomon*, first brought her national attention in 1977 after the story, about the life of a man named Macon "Milkman" Dead III discovering his heritage, was selected for the national Book of the Month Club. A little more than a decade later, in 1988, she won the Pulitzer Prize for Fiction for *Beloved*, the story of an enslaved woman who flees her captors only to face the ultimate sacrifice when she is captured once more. Two more novels in the *Beloved* trilogy followed, *Jazz* (1992) and *Paradise* (1997). She received the Presidential Medal of Freedom and the Nobel Prize in Literature (1993), served as the Robert F. Goheen Professor in the Humanities at Princeton University, and earned a lifetime's worth of honorary degrees. After her death, in 2019, a memorial tribute was held where luminaries such as Oprah Winfrey and Fran Lebowitz read eulogies.

"Writing fiction makes me feel completely and totally free," Morrison told *Glamour*. "I relish my other obligations—mothering my children, being a good friend—but this is the place where nobody tells me what to do."

"I WAS TO BE WILLING TO TAKE RISKS."

"The expectations of me were very high," Toni Morrison said as she accepted her 2007 Glamour *Woman of the Year* lifetime achievement award. "My job was to make sure that whatever gifts I had were not wasted."

One of the most celebrated writers of the 21st century, Morrison earned a Pulitzer Prize and a Nobel Prize in Literature, and her works are some of the most frequently taught in schools across the country. More than that, Morrison has inspired generations of young Black women to know that their words can—and will—make a difference in the world.

When Morrison took the stage that night in November, she started by addressing the young women in the audience: "I encourage you to pay very, very close attention to the abundance of possibilities on display on this stage and to the wide variety of routes that make those possibilities become reality." Here, her words .

BEING HERE AMONG FRIENDS

and colleagues and people I respect for a number of reasons, many of which have been described here, for me bears witness to an amazing phenomenon, and it's been a long time coming. I have borne witness for 60 years to the changes in women's lives, the unapologetic and the unfrenzied rise of women to responsible places in public.

I have to say that my own background is humble only in one respect, and that is money. In every other way it was rich in expectations. I think I am probably the last of that generation of African American families who, if they had a choice and there was only one choice, they educated their girls rather than their boys. And the boys did not complain about that. The reason was the instinct of survival. If they had a girl and a boy in the family, or two boys and two girls, they pushed the girls to get the degrees because a girl could take nurturing jobs. Teacher. Nurse. Maybe even physician. But whatever she did would be maternal. If they pushed their boys to get degrees, they would be in competition with white men.

So in order to protect the cell, so to speak, they chose that route. That is no longer true, thankfully, but it was a very strong characteristic in my youth. Therefore, the expectations of me were very high. Very high. And also taken for granted. Early on I was made aware of the genuinely life-threatening situations and circumstances my family had encountered and survived. Early on it was made clear to me that there was no haven, there was no safety, and I was not supposed to look for it. I was to be willing to risk. I was to be willing to step outside the gate that others had constructed for me.

My job was to make sure that whatever gifts I had were not wasted, were not compromised, and were not a cause for protected status. My job was to recognize integrity in other people and to try as best I could to develop it in myself. I thought the whole thing was unfair and outrageous, a burden I could not possibly bear.

I remember spending, I think, an inordinate amount of time in creativity resisting it. Yet as I grew older, the weight they put on me became a ballast, and the demands they made on me became a template. In a world that seemed increasingly hostile and chaotic, that was a lifeline. I had, and I still have, trouble, lots of trouble, meeting many of those standards, but I was always aware that the point was a journey and not the destination. Not only to save and live my life—because those people who had the courage and abiding sense of their own worth, as opposed to their value, assumed that my efforts would be no less than theirs.

So my place on this stage is a suggestion that those who put their trust in me have not yet been embarrassed.

Christiane Amanpour

WOMAN OF THE YEAR 2005

Christiane Amanpour has made it her career mission to expose, as she called it, "the worst that humanity has to offer." As an international correspondent and anchor for CNN and ABC, Amanpour has covered just about every major crisis you can think of—war, genocide, natural disasters, bombings, and pandemics—from the ground. She has conducted exclusive, insightful interviews with leaders around the world. But when her son asked what she did, she would tell him, "[I'm] fighting the bad guys and helping people who need help."

It's an accurate description: By shining a much-needed light on atrocities and wrongdoings, Amanpour has given a voice to the underrepresented people who have suffered. But when Amanpour gave an emotional delivery while reporting on the Bosnian War, many critics questioned her ability to remain objective. Amanpour pushed back: "Objectivity," she said, "can almost border on immorality."

As a journalist, Amanpour is not a passive observer of the world's atrocities—she passionately reports the truth in the hope that it can create meaningful change. It's why *Glamour* chose to honor her in 2005, a particularly grueling year in which she covered tsunami relief efforts, the London bombings, Hurricane Katrina, and the war in Iraq. "Americans have a need to know—they have a *right* to know," she said. "And I really do believe that by shining a spotlight on the world's most evil stories, you can help stop them."

Mariah Carey

WOMAN OF THE YEAR 1998

"What I've learned over the years is that I can trust my instincts," Mariah Carey said. Just a few things those instincts have led to: the record for most number-one singles by a solo artist, five Grammy Awards, a place in the Songwriters Hall of Fame, over 200 million records sold worldwide, and unquestionable status as one of the most influential artists of all time.

For years Carey's critics would whisper that her ex-husband, former Sony Music head Tommy Mottola, was the reason for her success. (He had famously "discovered" her when she was 19.) This despite the fact that the singer had written most of her own music. Despite the fact that she had coproduced all of her albums. Despite the fact that she has an extraordinary *five-octave* vocal range that few singers have ever matched. So when Carey and Mottola divorced in 1998—they had married in 1993, when she was 23 and he was 44—the singer used her newfound independence as a chance to prove everyone wrong. *Butterfly,* her first album in this new chapter, came with a more mature sound and image. It was an instant commercial success—and a major turning point in her life and career.

"I don't take anything for granted," Carey said. "I am grateful for everything that happens to me."

"There's never been a time in my life that I haven't been on a quest for music," Mariah Carey told *Glamour* in 1998.

Diane von Furstenberg

WOMAN OF THE YEAR 2005

There's a story Diane von Furstenberg loves to tell: In 1976, when the designer was 29 years old, a man sitting next to her on a plane asked, "What's a pretty girl like you doing reading the *Wall Street Journal*?" The answer: She was on the front page.

But she chose not to articulate that out loud. Instead, Furstenberg ignored him—it would have been too easy, she wrote in her book *The Woman I Wanted to Be*, and it was more satisfying to keep her triumph to herself. The feature, of course, was celebrating Furstenberg's fashion empire, launched four years earlier and built on the back of her groundbreaking knitted wrap dress, which in 1974 had changed the game for working women around the world. A *Newsweek* article dubbed her "the most marketable woman in fashion since Coco Chanel."

"I became a woman in charge," Furstenberg told *Glamour*. "And I used the confidence I had gained to give confidence to other women through a little dress."

In the decades following, Furstenberg's business had its share of highs and lows. Facing debts and overexposure after over-licensing her name, she sold the business and took a step back until returning to the spotlight in 1992 with a QVC line. It was a gamble—she was the first major designer to sell on TV—but she sold $1.3 million in her first two hours on air, giving her the confidence to relaunch her company a few years later. Furstenberg's return was even bigger than her first chapter; by 2005, when *Glamour* honored her as a Woman of the Year, she had just won the coveted lifetime achievement award from the Council of Fashion Designers of America.

Since then, Furstenberg's focus has been on helping women find confidence beyond the clothes they wear. "My future is much smaller because I'm an older woman, but I want to be able to use my knowledge, my wisdom, my connections, my experience, my voice in order to help other women be the women they want to be. That's my goal." The DVF Awards, created in 2010 and supported by her family's foundation, honors women who are dedicated to helping other women and gives nonprofits $50,000 to further their work. Not bad for a "pretty girl" on a plane.

"My mother, a Holocaust survivor, taught me, don't be afraid of your strength," Diane von Furstenberg told *Glamour* in 2005. "Enjoy it."

WHAT FIVE DECADES IN CHARGE HAS TAUGHT ME

As a young woman, Diane von Furstenberg—or as she prefers, DVF—knew one thing:
"I wanted to be a woman in charge," she told Glamour. *"I wanted to be able to have a man's life in a woman's*
body. I wanted to be able to have ideas. I wanted to be able to be self-sufficient and be free."
She accomplished all of this, redefining in the process what it means to be a visionary leader.
Here DVF shares what she's learned in five decades.

LEADERSHIP IS A COMMITMENT TO YOURSELF.

"If you own your imperfections, they become your assets. If you own your vulnerability, it becomes your strength. You constantly have to reinvent yourself. It never stops. Everyone always goes through difficult moments, and you just own it. Not being delusional is important. It's hard and it's difficult, but it's important."

SUCCESS IS LIKE HAPPINESS– IT DOESN'T STAY STILL.

"I lived an American dream. I was a big deal at 25 years old—cover of *Newsweek*, front page of the *Wall Street Journal*. But when everybody looks at you like you're on the top of the world, you know it's not quite as shiny as it seems to be. I had saturated the market. I knew I was in difficulty. The same happens when people think you've failed. That isn't true, because you already are taking steps to change that."

YOU HAVE NO CHOICE BUT TO GET THROUGH DIFFICULT MOMENTS.

"Sometimes you just want to make a hole in your bed and not get up. But you do. Live your difficult moments. Don't hide them. Don't blame. Take it in your hands. My mother was a big part of my strength. She survived the Holocaust, 13 months of captivity in Auschwitz. I was born 19 months later. She taught me that fear was not an option."

IT'S NATURAL TO DOUBT YOURSELF.

"When you doubt your power, you give power to your doubts. I doubt myself all the time. Everybody does. Only losers don't feel like losers. When people look at you and think, Oh, you're so together, that doesn't mean you feel that way at that moment. You have to live the adventure of your life as a journey. Live every moment, and take responsibility."

EXPAND YOUR UNIVERSE.

"Pay attention to people. [Even if you think] somebody is not interesting, they may mean something to your life. When I was 20 or 21, I met an Italian man who owned a printing mill. I didn't think I would learn anything from him, but it turned out everything I experienced there was important. I learned how to make a color palette, how to make color balance, the different techniques of printing…. Spend quality time with people you normally would not. You'll expand their universe, but the chances are they will expand yours too."

BE YOURSELF. ALWAYS.

"The more yourself you are, the more confident you will be. People will see that. It all depends on you. You could lose your health, your wealth, your family, even your freedom, but you never lose your character. Building character comes from being really honest with yourself. Like yourself, but be strict with yourself."

Billie Jean King

WOMAN OF THE YEAR 2006

Billie Jean King may have 39 Grand Slam titles, a Presidential Medal of Freedom, and a national tennis center named after her, but the tennis champion's true legacy will be the pioneering work she's done for equality and social justice.

In 2006 *Glamour* celebrated her with a lifetime achievement award for being such a committed advocate for equal rights. Just a few examples of how she's paved the way for others: King has demanded equal prize money for women in sports, served as the first president of the first player's union for women (the Women's Tennis Association), founded the Women's Sports Foundation, and lobbied Congress for Title IX legislation, which protects people from discrimination in sports and academics.

And, of course, there was her 1973 victory over self-proclaimed "male chauvinist" and former top tennis player Bobby Riggs in the famed "Battle of the Sexes." He believed the women's game was so inferior that he could beat a top woman player, even at the age of 55. King defeated him in three straight sets in front of a global television audience of 90 million. For King the cultural impact of the match was even greater than the win. "I've had grown men come up to me in tears," she said. "They'll say, 'When I was 10, I saw that match and raise my daughters differently now.'"

Her work supporting and inspiring women didn't stop with that match. King's leadership initiative, founded in 2014, has been dedicated to moving the needle on issues affecting inclusion in the workplace. "To me," she explained, "true champions lift up others."

Katie Couric

WOMAN OF THE YEAR 1992, 2002, AND 2006

In 2000, *Today Show* cohost Katie Couric invited millions of viewers into the exam room for her colonoscopy—a mundane, routine appointment that she turned into something absolutely revolutionary. Long before Twitter and Instagram made oversharing an expected form of communication, Couric's openness was unheard of—and its impact was immediate. In addition to it raising massive awareness—her husband, Jay Monahan, had died of colorectal cancer two years earlier—doctors saw a 20 percent jump in screenings nationwide. They called it "the Couric effect."

"We never know what kind of circumstances we'll face in our lifetimes, and I think that's one of life's great mysteries," Couric said as she accepted her award in 2002 for her lifesaving work. (It was her second time winning—the first, in 1992, was for joining *Today* as an anchor.) "But, of course, when you do, it's how you handle them that truly defines who you are.... I think any of you who occupied my chair on *The Today Show* would have done what I have done: inform people about a disease that destroyed my family but not our spirit."

Anyone may have made that same choice, but few have the reach Couric does. In every role the broadcast journalist has taken on—anchor of *CBS Evening News*, correspondent for *60 Minutes*, and host of her own talk show, *Katie*, among them—she connects with viewers and interview subjects through her warm, uplifting spirit. The last to interview John F. Kennedy Jr. before his death in 1999 and the first to speak on-air with pilot Chesley Sullenberger after the "Miracle on the Hudson" plane landing, Couric has received numerous accolades for her journalistic integrity. It's why *Glamour* honored her for a WOTY Award again, in 2006, for her bold move to CBS to become America's first solo woman anchor.

What's most important to Couric than any résumé achievement, though, is what young women in her audience take away. "We are role models for people [who are] watching, and I want young women watching to understand that I do consider myself a feminist. That I'm proud of that. A lot of little girls see me and say, 'I can do that.' I want them to see that I'm assertive, independent, and responsible." For that reason, *Glamour* is proud to have honored Couric as a Woman of the Year a record three times.

Katie Couric is the only Woman of the Year to be honored three times.

"It's not ho
with succe
measure o
It's how
with the

w you deal
ss that's the
f a woman.
you deal
setbacks."

—KATIE COURIC, WOMAN OF THE YEAR 1992, 2002, AND 200

Iman

Iman Abdulmajid said the seed was planted for the creation of her world-dominating beauty brand Iman Cosmetics in 1976. She was on set for a *Vogue* shoot—one of her first jobs after coming to the United States from Nairobi, Kenya. She was brand-new to the industry, and it was only her third day in New York City, but the Somali-born model was still surprised when the makeup artist asked if she had brought her own foundation because he had nothing for her. (He did not ask the white model on set the same question.) When Iman said she did not, the makeup artist mixed a concoction. When she finally looked in the mirror, Iman was mortified. "My skin looked gray," she said in a *Glamour* interview. "I decided I was going to create something for myself that I would be able to take to shoots, so nobody will ever catch me unprepared again."

Iman, who was married to musician David Bowie for 24 years until his death in 2016, went on to have a massively successful modeling career—she served as a muse to respected designers like Yves Saint Laurent, landed major contracts with brands like Revlon, and became a household name. But after nearly two decades of bringing her own makeup to sets and mixing products to match her skin tone, she wanted to launch a cosmetics and skincare collection for women of color. Founded in 1994, Iman Cosmetics was revolutionary: With few mainstream options available for women with dark skin tones, her line filled a much-needed space in the marketplace. By the time Iman was honored as *Glamour*'s Woman of the Year in 2006, it was a multimillion-dollar business. "I believe a woman can be all about lipstick or prefer nothing but soap and water—but what ultimately matters is that you act on your dreams, great or small."

She was also recognized in 2006 for her nonprofit work on the AIDS crisis in Africa, where she had partnered with Keep a Child Alive (KCA) to fund antiretroviral drugs for children there. Her philanthropy has defined much of the past two decades of her life; she has advocated for Save the Children while continuing to fight poverty and social injustice with humanitarian organization UNICEF. "It's the most important work I've ever done," she told *Glamour*.

Iman at her Iman
Cosmetics offices
in New York City.

"I'm still afraid, I'm still vulnerable, I still punk out, but I'm living my truth in abundance all the time," Solange Knowles told *Glamour* in 2017.

Solange Knowles

WOMAN OF THE YEAR 2017

If there's a roadmap to success, as they say, Solange Knowles doesn't want to see it. "Anything truly monumental that has helped me grow and evolve," she said, "I've had to be uncomfortable to go through it."

For her that meant embracing every life experience—good and bad—as it came. Creative from the start, the artist began writing songs as early as nine and got her first taste of touring as a backup dancer for her sister Beyoncé's group, Destiny's Child. By 16 she had released her first album, *Solo Star*. The following years were a different kind of journey for Solange— she married her high school sweetheart at 17, gave birth to her son at 18, moved to Idaho, and took a career break—but after her divorce in 2007, she started writing music again. This time, now in her 20s, her work was more personal, more mature. Critics and fans alike took notice. But it was her 2016 release of *A Seat at the Table* that was a watershed moment for Solange as an artist, as she sang about cultural appropriation, racism, activism, and empowerment. The album was considered a groundbreaking piece of work, and it won a Grammy for the song "Cranes in the Sky."

Her success was hard-won. "We live in a society where there is this 'glow-up' concept," Solange said, "but I can't think of anyone who's had a glow-up story and hasn't put in the work." All women, she said, experience self-doubt. Freedom comes when they embrace it. "I fully encourage women to stand in their truths, their flaws, and their complications," she said. "I don't think anyone can tell your story better than you."

"I'M NOT AFRAID, FOR I KNOW THAT FEAR IS UGLY."

When Solange Knowles took the stage at the 2017 Glamour Women of the Year Awards, *she delivered a poetic speech about art, fear, and empowerment. Though it was about her own personal journey, her words are a mission statement all women can get behind.*

WHEN I WAS ABOUT 11 YEARS OLD, someone said to me, "You've got to shoot for the moon. Even if you miss, you'll land amongst the stars." Well, I wasn't interested in either. I was interested in the journey there. How does one shoot for the moon? Do they just levitate as a celestial being? Or do they get there by a mothership? Did these stars find each other before they became constellations, or did they slowly evolve into the divine beings that they are by just existing? And were they afraid? As I've journeyed into my own evolution, I'm grateful I never found the answers. And I'm grateful I probably never will. I simply stopped needing to know.

I think we as women are told from the second that we come into our own that we not only need to be shooting for the moon, but that we must hold the moon in the palms of our hands, turn it until the sun comes to morning, nurture all of it, and look and feel like a goddess with crowning glory while doing so. And that has not been my journey. My journey has been a rise and fall. It's been ugly. It's been loud. It's been disruptive. It's been long. It's often been painful. But it's been free, it's been beautiful, and it's been mine.

This past year has been one of the most rewarding and wonderful moments of my life. I was able to turn my pain and my trauma and my rage into work and into my art. And I have been filled with a gratitude so abundant that I can't even express it in words how thankful I am. I'm eternally grateful, and I will never ever take for granted the way people have uplifted me for my voice and my work. I want to thank *Glamour* from the bottom of my heart for the fact that the women you have chosen to be these Women of the Year are moving mountains and shaking the ground beneath us all. And I also want to thank the women who are just being. Just existing every day in their own truths, whatever that may be. That is as radical as anything.

Thank you for giving a voice to a woman like me, who might not be your graceful, poised, polite, soft, and gentle woman and may never strive to be. For letting the world know that there's room for both. For not turning your back on me when I'm passionate, when I'm loud, when you get emails from me telling you I disagree when I want to have control of my body and create spaces for those who look and feel like me. For when I need to learn to shut up and not say or do dumb shit and to know when to choose my battles. They can't all be battles, and sometimes I need to think before I speak, and put my Twitter fingers in *time the hell out.*

As I look around the room, I feel so completely and utterly honored and humbled to be amongst women like these, who gave me a voice when my voice may have cracked when I tried to raise it. Who gave me a language when I was struggling to speak my own.

The last few weeks have been very difficult for me personally, to say the least, as I've embarked on a new set of challenges before for me. But I'm not afraid, for I know that fear is ugly. Fear has no face; it stares at you from many dimensions, but its worst angle is dead-on. I'm looking forward to the day that I greet fear wholeheartedly, nose to nose, and tell it, "You have met your goddamn match." I want to continue to live up to this moment. I'll cherish it forever. And I just want to say thank you to Black women especially for uplifting me and loving up on me and seeing me in a way that I might not have even seen myself. I will continue to lift our voices.

Nora Ephron

WOMAN OF THE YEAR 1993

After Nora Ephron graduated from Wellesley College, in 1962, she applied for a writing job at *Newsweek*. But, she was told, the magazine didn't hire women writers. She had to settle for a position in the mailroom instead.

Fortunately, the author and filmmaker overcame that sexist roadblock and went on to become one of the most influential voices of a generation. In all her books (including *Heartburn, I Remember Nothing*) and movies (*When Harry Met Sally, You've Got Mail*), Ephron delivers insightful truths wrapped in sparkling, witty dialogue. ("Never marry a man you wouldn't want to be divorced from," she once quipped.) One of her most beloved movies, *Sleepless in Seattle*, was co-written and directed by Ephron and premiered the year she was honored with a WOTY.

There are many quotable lines in Ephron's catalog of classics, but the most cited after her death, in 2012, was a commencement speech she gave at her alma mater, Wellesley College, in 1996. At that year's WOTY ceremony, *Glamour* asked Cynthia Nixon and Mamie and Grace Gummer to read a selection. Though it was written 16 years earlier, her words remained as true as ever. "Above all, be the heroine of your life," she wrote. "This is the season when a clutch of successful women—who have it all—give speeches to women like you and say, to be perfectly honest, you can't have it all...but in case any of you are wondering, of course you can have it all. What are you going to do? Everything, is my guess. It will be a little messy, but embrace the mess. It will be complicated, but rejoice in the complications. It will not be anything like what you think it will be like, but surprises are good for you. And don't be frightened: You can always change your mind. I know: I've had four careers and three husbands."

Nora Ephron's words of wisdom: "Above all, be the heroine of your life."

Donatella Versace

WOMAN OF THE YEAR 2010

When Jennifer Lopez wore a green, leaf-printed dress to the 2000 Grammys that Donatella Versace had designed, the low-cut look caused such a stir that Google Images was later created to keep up with the search demand. Now *that* is power.

Versace, the brand and the woman, has always been synonymous with this kind of bold, unabashed confidence. She started her career as an influence on her brother Gianni, who founded the label in 1978. But after his murder in 1997, Versace was suddenly tasked with running a major luxury label while processing her grief. "I had to hide my pain," she said about that challenging time. "I could never be alone and cry."

Versace found her footing and became a staple for celebrities looking to make a statement on the red carpet. (See: Lopez and that green dress.) *Glamour* honored her with a Woman of the Year Award in 2010 after the company had reached a milestone period of growth, both artistically and financially. Sales were exceeding projections at the 80-plus boutiques open from Las Vegas to Shanghai, and Versace was critically acclaimed for her "superiority" in design, as the *New York Times* noted. "I am feeling so free to express myself creatively," she told *Glamour* at the time. "I've found my strength."

Though the brand was sold in 2018 to Michael Kors Holdings and renamed Capri Holdings, Versace stayed on as head of creative design—a testament to her enduring legacy. After the coronavirus pandemic deeply affected her home country of Italy, and the fashion industry at large, Versace donated hundreds of thousands of dollars to relief efforts and gave up her 2021 salary. When asked about this momentous act, Versace answered with characteristic flair. "Everyone does what they can."

Madonna

WOMAN OF THE YEAR 1990

In 1990 *Glamour* debuted the first-ever Women of the Year Awards, and Madonna—fresh off the success of "Like a Prayer" and *Dick Tracy*—was selected to be its cover star. Editor in chief Ruth Whitney summed up the power of Madonna best at the awards ceremony that November:

"Madonna Louise Veronica Ciccone knew exactly what she wanted when she left Michigan for New York City at the tender age of 19. While everyone's a celebrity for 15 minutes and media stars come and go, Madonna is still getting what she wanted, still on center stage, still top banana, still commander in chief of her own wildly successful enterprise. Through her self-reliance and her ability to evolve a fresh and timely image, Madonna is as hot as ever, and we admire her for it. She pushes the limits of our cultural restrictions, toying with taboo. She opens us to a joyous celebration of creativity, whether it's through songs and lyrics, video imagery, a cameo role in a Broadway play, or as the slinky Breathless Mahoney in *Dick Tracy*. Her energy and her imagination reshape the stereotypes that have kept women trapped in their cultural roles. Woman of the Year: Madonna."

Those same words could still be applied to Madonna three decades later as she remains as commanding a creative force as ever. Case in point: After her single "I Don't Search I Find" topped Billboard's dance club chart in 2020, she became the first—and only—artist to have a number-one song five decades in a row. So to honor Madonna and her immense contribution to reshaping womanhood and self-empowerment, we are sharing the star's cover again here.

Madonna, photographed here in 1990, was one of *Glamour*'s first Women of the Year.

how to use your voice

For 30 years, Glamour has honored bold, barrier-breaking women who stand up and speak out in order to make a difference. These Women of the Year come from vastly different backgrounds, but they all share one thing in common: They inspire us. How will they inspire you?

TO CHANGE THE WORLD

DO YOUR RESEARCH.

"You can't disrupt what you don't understand. But once you understand, perhaps you engage with these things differently, no matter who you are."
—AVA DUVERNAY, WOMAN OF THE YEAR 2019

SHARE YOUR EXPERIENCE.

"When a person is going through hell, and she encounters someone who went through hellish hell and survived, then she can say: Mine is not so bad as all that. She came through, and so can I."
—MAYA ANGELOU, WOMAN OF THE YEAR 2009

TAKE CARE OF YOURSELF—AND REMEMBER THAT THE *REAL* WORK IS ON THE LISTENER.

"Sometimes being a survivor means drinking enough water and sleeping well at night. Just facing the day can require courage. Fight, but just as important, rest. It's society that needs to do more, to learn how to listen, to hold the space for survivors and hold perpetrators accountable."
—CHANEL MILLER, WOMAN OF THE YEAR 2016

WORDS HAVE MEANING, BUT THEY'RE NOT ABSOLUTE.

"I feel like a bumper car because if I go and hit a block wall, I just go back, I just go in another direction. What I would want for you girls, and what I would want for everyone, especially women, is that you don't take no for an answer. *No* is just some bullshit word that someone made up."
—CHER, WOMAN OF THE YEAR 2010

FIND OTHERS WITH COMMON GOALS.

"We, as Americans, as women, and as sisters, have an opportunity to join together to turn the volume up on love."
—JANELLE MONÁE, WOMAN OF THE YEAR 2018

AND MOST OF ALL, JUST DO.

"You hardly need my words of encouragement, young women, because you are creating your own words and encouraging one another. Because of you, we oldies have hope for the real world. So go for it."
—MARGARET ATWOOD, WOMAN OF THE YEAR 2019

Ava DuVernay

WOMAN OF THE YEAR 2019

If you're ever concerned about making a career pivot, consider this: Having spent years working as a film publicist, Ava DuVernay didn't pick up a video camera until she was 32. The rest was literally history—in 2016, with two narrative feature films under her belt, DuVernay became the first Black woman to be nominated by the Academy as a director in a feature category. She then became the first to direct a $100 million–grossing film with 2018's *A Wrinkle in Time*. When *Glamour* honored her as a WOTY in 2019, her Netflix limited series *When They See Us* was receiving widespread acclaim for its moving and timely portrayal of the 1989 Central Park jogger case in which five Black and Latino men were wrongly accused of raping a white woman. It received a record 16 Emmy nominations for writing, acting, and directing.

Through her own production and distribution company, Array, DuVernay has continued to create opportunities for underrepresented storytellers. One example: Only women directors have been hired to shoot her television series *Queen Sugar,* about the lives of three siblings who come together. DuVernay doesn't want a seat at the table, she explained. "I want the table to be rebuilt in my likeness and in the likeness of others long forced out of the room."

By disrupting the outdated systems that Hollywood—and America at large—have upheld, DuVernay has created real, lasting change on-screen and off. Don't accept just a chair, DuVernay taught us: Take the whole damn table.

"Sixteen Emmy nominations is not what I think of when I think of *When They See Us,*" Ava DuVernay told *Glamour* in 2019. "I think of the day that the men wept in my arms and I wept in theirs as they told me that I told their story better than they could have imagined."

"I don't want table or even half. I want th rebuilt in my in the likene long forced o

ss of others
ut of the room."

—AVA DUVERNAY, WOMAN OF THE YEAR 2019

The Women of 'Saturday Night Live'

WOMEN OF THE YEAR 2002

It took close to three decades, but the *Saturday Night Live* cast finally reached something close to gender parity in 2002 when five of the 11 repertory players were women: Tina Fey, Ana Gasteyer, Maya Rudolph, Rachel Dratch, and Amy Poehler.

It was absolutely revolutionary to finally have some much-needed woman energy break up the show's boys'-club history. Skits about mom jeans, baby bumps, and Botox were no longer off-limits. "It's nice not to run out of bodies when doing a skit about *The View*," Fey joked at the time about spoofing the long-running all-women daytime talk show. Greater than that, the five showed the power—and true marketability—of women in comedy. And then they leveled up again, carving a new path through hit movies (*Mean Girls, Bridesmaids*), best-selling books (*Bossypants*), and beloved TV series (*Parks and Recreation*). They also opened the door for future *SNL* stars like Kristen Wiig and Leslie Jones to become household names.

"You know, our job is to reflect and parody the world around us," Gasteyer said as she accepted the *Glamour* Woman of the Year Award on behalf of the group. "There are women everywhere available to be parodied—for us, it's become an extremely easy job to do."

"Some women advance the cause through courage, legislation, and innovation," she continued. "Others do it with fart jokes and perm wigs."

From left: Tina Fey, Ana Gasteyer, Maya Rudolph, Rachel Dratch, and Amy Poehler.

Selena Gomez

WOMAN OF THE YEAR 2012

What makes someone a *Glamour* Woman of the Year is never about the level of fame they've reached or how many chart-topping singles they've produced. It's how they use their platform that matters. See: Selena Gomez.

She's been in the spotlight since she was 15 and starring in the Disney Channel's *Wizards of Waverly Place*. For Gomez—at one point the most followed woman on Instagram—that meant endless scrutiny about her personal life and an exhausting schedule. But she was honored as a WOTY in 2012 for her amazing work with UNICEF, with which Gomez has held an active role since 2009, when she was 17.

Years after her Woman of the Year Award, Gomez also became an important advocate for mental health. After seeking treatment for anxiety and depression in 2014, the singer spoke out about mental health issues and in 2020 shared her own bipolar disorder diagnosis and mental health journey. "I grew up in one of the biggest high schools in the world, and that's the Disney Channel," she said. "Everybody was falling in love with each other or not liking each other, and it was exhausting... and now I'm so opinionated, and I don't have time for the cattiness. I have good people around me, and I'm glad I'm at the place I'm in. I wish I was there back then."

It's not just about Gomez's journey, though—she's also been a role model for her young fan base. "If I had let all of the negative stuff affect me, I don't think I would be satisfied with the person I am now," she said. "That's what I tell my fans: If you're miserable with everything going on in school, that is so not going to matter the moment you leave. My mom always told me, 'Just turn the other cheek and keep moving forward.' That's something I've always done, and now I look back and I have no regrets."

When Selena Gomez accepted her WOTY Award in 2012, she offered this advice to all the young girls in the audience: "You have a voice. You have a chance to just do what you love."

Chrissy Teigen

WOMAN OF THE YEAR 2018

There is no topic off-limits for model, host, and cookbook author Chrissy Teigen—and that's what makes her a *Glamour* Woman of the Year. Whether she's joking about stretch marks or sharing a political takedown so scathing that President Donald Trump blocks her on Twitter, Teigen is always one thing: authentic.

That ability to throw off the glossy sheen of Hollywood and stay true to her-self inspires women around the world—and because she has been so honest with fans and critics alike, her achievements and journey feel somehow personal to us as well.

But never has her raw openness spoken more to women than when she revealed in her 2017 *Glamour* cover story that she had postpartum depression after giving birth to her daughter, Luna. "I have a great

life," she wrote in her essay. "But post-partum does not discriminate. I couldn't control it. And that's part of the reason it took me so long to speak up: I felt selfish, icky, and weird saying aloud that I'm struggling. Sometimes I still do."

The story struck a nerve—according to Teigen, it's the thing women ask her about the most. For using her platform to speak so honestly about such a sensitive and impor-tant topic, and for her deep commitment to authentic representation of celebrity, *Glamour* honored her as Woman of the Year a year later. For Teigen it was never a ques-tion of whether to share her experience. As always she knew she just needed to be real. "If people are ever feeling bullied or down, I think it's just absolutely crucial to stay true to yourself," she said. "Someone's gonna appreciate you for exactly how you are."

Don't be afraid of risks: "When I look at the most successful people around me, I feel like they all had plans," Chrissy Teigen told *Glamour*. "But I never had a plan. Never."

Mindy Kaling

WOMAN OF THE YEAR 2014

Describing all that is Mindy Kaling— talented actor, writer, director, author, producer, and mother included—is tough, but her *Office* costar Ellie Kemper got close: "She's like an honor-roll student-athlete ninja warrior."

In everything Kaling has done, there is a deep understanding and humor about what it means to be a woman. Binge-watch her beloved series *The Mindy Project*, for which *Glamour* honored her with a 2014 Woman of the Year Award. Read her two *New York Times* best-selling memoirs *Is Everyone Hanging Out Without Me? (and Other Concerns)* and *Why Not Me?* Watch *Late Night*, the Amazon movie so good it scored a cool $13 million deal at Sundance, one of the biggest sales in the film festival's history. In all you will find a unique ability to put into words something so deeply relatable that you feel like it was plucked straight from your brain—just funnier.

For Kaling, though, her work is personal. "I've always felt that I represent the underdog," she said. "As an Indian woman and a single mom, I've felt like the kind of person who often does not get to be the lead of a story. I want the stories that I tell, the characters I play and create, to resonate with people who do not see themselves onscreen."

She continued, "When I'm gone and people look at my body of work, they can see it in the context of where I came from and where my family came from and say, 'Wow, that was the beginning of a ripple effect'—that people are inspired because they felt that I, in some way, helped move the door open a couple more inches. That would be really incredible to me."

Mindy Kaling's words to live by: "When it comes to decision-making, be your own best friend. I remember really well when my mom said that to me, the day before she died [in 2012]. She was giving me comfort. It's been very useful in so many situations."

1998

Editor in Chief

Ruth Whitney

1967

Ruth Whitney, pictured here with civil rights activist Myrlie Evers-Williams and actor Glenn Close, was editor in chief of *Glamour* from 1967 to 1998.

THERE WOULD BE NO WOMEN OF THE YEAR WITHOUT RUTH *Whitney. The* Glamour *awards were her and senior editor Judith Daniels's brainchild, developed after decades of Whitney celebrating and supporting the achievements of women while she was editor in chief. Under Whitney's leadership, the magazine broke new ground through her innovative mix of politics, style, and service. A year into her tenure,* Glamour *became the first fashion magazine to feature a Black woman on its cover. She also led the publication to four prestigious National Magazine Awards, including one for a series conceived by Whitney on abortion access in America. When she died of Lou Gehrig's disease, in June 1999, the loss was immeasurable. At that year's award ceremony, Katie Couric delivered a moving tribute to the legendary editor, an excerpt of which follows.*

"In 1967, when Ruth arrived at Glamour, *it was a glossy magazine for genteel ladies who wore hats, heels, and white gloves. But not for long. As the pill, the sexual revolution, and feminism altered the way women lived, Ruth changed the way women looked at the world and looked at themselves. She had guts, she had style, and beneath her beautifully tailored suits, the heart of a rebel. She encouraged her editors to break big stories about once verboten topics by packaging substantial news among the 'girly stuff.' She raised our collective consciousness in an unprecedented way. Today's* Glamour *is the legacy of her 31 years as editor in chief. When she died of Lou Gehrig's disease, Ruth had more than surpassed her stated goal: to make women feel good about themselves. As we pay tribute to winners past and present, we also honor a timeless and tireless champion of us all."*

Here, 30 years after Women of the Year began, Ruth's son, Philip Whitney, remembers his mother—and her impact on generations of women.

The process of selecting the Women of the Year was very secretive. My mother would go into her office at home with the door closed to call each individual to tell them they had been selected. But I remember there were conversations with my dad in 1991 about the importance of including Anita Hill after her testimony to the Senate Judiciary Committee about Supreme Court nominee Clarence Thomas and how that was an absolute must for my mom. In order to include her in the issue, they had to hold the press for the magazine.

When I met Anita Hill at the Women of the Year Awards ceremony that year, I was 28 and terrified and excited to meet this incredibly brave woman who had stood up to the entire political apparatus of the United States to tell the truth. For me that was an honor beyond all honors. That moment will always be burned into my memory more than anything else.

One of the things my mom always debated and discussed was finding a balance among the honorees: She wanted to avoid the obvious celebrity choices and instead look for women from business, entertainment, politics, nonprofits, and more who were doing really important work. Some were kind of toiling in obscurity, and it was *those* women she wanted to track down to spotlight their achievements.

My mom used habit to her advantage. Every night she left the office at 350 Madison Avenue and took the 5:10 train to be home by 6:00. She would enjoy a martini, make dinner, and then, when all was quiet, sit down on the living room sofa with piles of manuscripts and mail from readers. She read every single letter, sometimes discussing them, both the effusively positive and the very critical, with my dad.

As I think back to those nightly rituals, I realize that they actually had a profound influence on me. I was a proud son—who would later become a grateful man—and thankful that I had her as my mother. In helping her readers, she was also helping me be a better person and feminist man. It's hard to convey how important those letters were to her, but it was that relationship with the readers—not the awards or the peer respect or the financial success, although they were certainly nice outcomes—that fueled her passion for *Glamour*. Like any good friendship, sometimes you have to listen and sometimes you have to tell. Perhaps the greatest secret to her success was that she knew instinctively when it was time to lead and when it was time to listen. That's why she took time every night to read that pile of letters.

Women of the Year was never considered by my mother to be a once-a-year event. She wanted to create a network of impressive women who would continue the connections they made at those awards over time. It's why she would invite past winners back—and many did return. If not every year, then as often as possible. The women who forged friendships and partnerships from the Women of the Year Awards—that is her legacy.

Janelle Monáe

WOMAN OF THE YEAR 2018

Janelle Monáe understood the power of words from an early age. She grew up in a working-class neighborhood of Kansas City, and her grandparents would share tales from their ancestors about those who escaped slavery during Bleeding Kansas, a violent period in the state's history before the Civil War began in 1861. "You can still see some of the ruins there," she said. "Just knowing that I come from a place where people were trying to be free and fighting for their survival, it makes me feel like I have a lot of people to make proud. I don't want their work and their blood and their sweat and their tears and their sacrifices to go in vain."

And so the singer and actor has spent her entire career sharing stories and voices of people who were once overlooked but deserved to be heard. The first single from her successful 2013 sophomore album, *The Electric Lady,* is titled "Q.U.E.E.N.," an acronym for marginalized people. (It stands for Queer community; Untouchables; Emigrants; Excommunicated; Negroid.) Three years later, she starred in *Hidden Figures* as real-life NASA mathematician and aeronautical engineer Mary Jackson. Even on the red carpet, Monáe was storytelling—she always wore black and white to pay homage to the working-class uniforms her parents and grandparents wore every day as janitors, postal workers, and trash collectors.

In 2018 *Glamour* honored Monáe as a Woman of the Year for her trailblazing album *Dirty Computer.* In the music video for the song "Pynk," Monáe wears a pair of pants shaped like vaginas. It went viral, naturally. "I've always taken issue with people trying to place an image on what a young girl could be," she said. "I was going to decide that for myself."

But perhaps there's no better way to sum up the magic of Monáe than the closing words of her Woman of the Year speech: "I come in peace, but I mean business."

"I've always taken issue with people trying to place an image on what a young girl could be," said Janelle Monáe. "I was going to decide that for myself."

"I'm not
piss o
abusers
I'm not

afraid to
ff the
of power.
afraid."

Vera Wang

WOMAN OF THE YEAR 2003

When Vera Wang got engaged and started shopping for a wedding dress, the former *Vogue* fashion editor was astonished. It was 1989, but the bridal industry hadn't evolved, in her opinion, since the 1950s. Everything she tried on seemed more suited to a little girl than a modern woman. Wang had a vision: a line of sophisticated gowns—sexy, but not vulgar—that would fill a hole in a very profitable marketplace.

Her instincts turned out to be spot-on. After her first bridal shop opened, in 1990, Wang built a fashion and lifestyle empire that by 2019 was worth an estimated $460 million. Her iconic wedding gowns have been worn by everyone from Kim Kardashian West to Alicia Keys to Chelsea Clinton. (In pop culture she's big too: Wang was one of several designers character Carrie Bradshaw wears in her *Vogue* spread in 2008's *Sex and the City* movie ahead of her wedding to "Big.") When *Glamour* honored Wang as a Woman of the Year in 2003, the designer had expanded into fragrance, eyewear, china, and crystal as well.

In her WOTY Award speech, Wang spoke on the importance of passion—"that special something that comes directly from the heart," as she put it—for success. It's a singular kind of inspiration, she said. Have passion for those we love. Passion for what we believe in. And lastly, passion for what we do.

"I design for women who live in the real world," Vera Wang told *Glamour* in 2003.

237

Robin Roberts

WOMAN OF THE YEAR 2014

Robin Roberts doesn't believe in bucket lists. As the *Good Morning America* coanchor said in her 2014 Woman of the Year profile interview, "Call it your 'do' list, and then go and do those things. Now."

It's sage advice from someone who has crossed a lot off her "do" list. The journalist's honest approach has made her a hit with viewers and interview subjects alike. When former president Barack Obama was ready to give a groundbreaking interview on his support for gay marriage, Roberts got the exclusive. With Roberts on board, *Good Morning America* surpassed *The Today Show* to become America's most-watched morning show in 2012.

The next year, Roberts returned from a nearly six-month leave for a bone marrow transplant. Almost 6.1 million people tuned in to welcome her back. Her openness about her health challenges—she has survived breast cancer and myelodysplastic syndromes (MDS), a life-threatening bone marrow disease—led to more than just higher ratings: Be the Match Registry, a nonprofit operated by the National Marrow Donor Program, saw an 1,800 percent boost in donors after Roberts encouraged viewers to sign up. By increasing awareness around bone marrow transplants, she saved lives, for which *Glamour* gave her a 2014 Woman of the Year Award.

At the event Roberts shared an inspiring message to all young people going through a hard time: "I know it seems like it's the end of the world, but know it's something that's going to make them so much stronger and better in the end."

The key, she added, is to focus on the now. "When I find myself becoming sad, it's because I'm living in the past. And when I become anxious, it's because I'm living in the future. It's only when I'm living in the present that I'm at peace."

Maya Angelou

WOMAN OF THE YEAR 2009

Maya Angelou lived such a full and interesting life, it took seven autobiographies to detail it all. But her most famous autobiography, *I Know Why the Caged Bird Sings*, is about her earliest years, and in it she details the racism and hardship she experienced growing up in southwestern Arkansas. Since its publication in 1969, her honest, unflinching account of the traumas she faced has moved generations of women looking to put to words their own pain. Taught in hundreds of English classes across the country, *I Know Why the Caged Bird Sings* has sold more than a million copies, never been out of print, and been translated into 17 languages.

Angelou's journey to becoming a best-selling author and poet was a winding road: She was the first Black cable car conductor in San Francisco at just 16. She gave birth to her son, Guy, at 17, and in her 20s she began working as a nightclub dancer and singer, at one point touring Europe in a production of *Porgy and Bess*. By the 1960s she was a dedicated civil rights activist working with Martin Luther King Jr. and Malcolm X. Even after she reached international acclaim as an author, Angelou kept reinventing herself—she served as a professor, director, and even created a line of Hallmark cards. Up until her death, in 2014, at 86, she was still writing. Her memorial service included speeches from Michelle Obama and Oprah Winfrey and was livestreamed so all who mourned the loss of the visionary could participate.

For Angelou, who was honored with the WOTY lifetime achievement award in 2009, showing empathy through her work was paramount—it was equal parts healing and inspiring. "When a person is going through hell," she said, "and she encounters someone who went through hellish hell and survived, then she can say, 'Mine is not so bad as all that. She came through, and so can I.'"

Maya Angelou was photographed at her home in Winston-Salem, North Carolina.

"WE ARE ALL PHENOMENAL."

When Maya Angelou was honored at the 2009 Women of the Year Awards,
the audience was expecting to hear something phenomenal. The poet, author, and civil rights activist
had, as former president Bill Clinton described in his introduction, "always found a way
to move both our minds and our hearts.... Maya Angelou is the very definition of phenomenal."

What the audience perhaps didn't expect was for Angelou to open with a poignant
gospel song. "When it look like the sun wasn't gonna shine anymore," she sang in her honeyed voice,
"God put a rainbow in the clouds."

The speech that followed was a stirring portrait of what connects us all as human beings.
It was so moving that when Rihanna was honored later in the evening, she said jokingly, "I have to say,
Maya Angelou, I love you, but you made this [speech] terribly more difficult for me."
Here, Angelou's words .

IMAGINE. IN GENESIS WE ARE TOLD that the rain had persisted so unrelentingly that people thought it would never cease, and in an attempt to put the people at ease, God put a rainbow in the sky. That's in the Bible. However, in the 19th century some African American slave poet lyricist—probably a woman, I'm not sure about that—said God put the rainbow not just in the sky but in the clouds themselves. We know that suns and moons and stars and all sorts of comets are in the sky, but clouds can go lower and lower so that the viewer cannot see the light. But if the light is put right into the clouds, it means in the meanest of times, in the cruelest of times, in the most threatening of times, there's a possibility of seeing hope. Women are rainbows in the clouds.

That's who we are. We are Black and white, we are Asian and Spanish-speaking Native American, we are Jewish, and we are Muslim. We are fat and thin, pretty and plain, gay and straight. This is who we are. We came here as multitaskers. Whether we came here in the filthy hatches of slave ships or whether we came here as brides to be bought, we came here. And that's who we are today.

That's who glamour is. I know that many people think glamour is superficial; it's just a surface of things, powder, little rouge. No, glamour is profound. Glamour says, "I have enough responsibility to take responsibility for myself and the time and the spaces I occupy." That's glamour, saying I want to be as beautiful as I can be to myself first and to anybody else who has enough sense to see me.

To be introduced tonight by my president, to be introduced tonight by women... this is to be in company where there's a rainbow in the clouds. And we need it just now, so I am grateful to be a woman. I am grateful to God. I must have done something right in another life to come here as a woman and to know enough to be a good sister, a good lover, a good wife, a good friend, a good daughter, a good buddy, a good niece to some men who know enough to value me. We are all phenomenal. I know you know that. And I know that you know that 98 percent of all the species which have lived on this little blob of spit and sand are now extinct because they got out of balance. We are still here, so that means we are still in balance. That men are as phenomenal as women. I will say just two things to the men: One, you have to know that. And two, you have to show it. There's a world of difference between being an old male and being a man. Being an old female and being a woman. I say to the men, you have to write your own point. To the women: Many people wonder where my secret lies. I'm not cute. Or built to suit a fashion model size. When you see me walking it ought to make you proud. I say it's in the reach of my arms. The span of my hips. The stride of my step. The curl of my lips. I am a woman. Phenomenally. Phenomenal woman. That's all you women here. That's all our grandmothers and great-grandmothers. Our great-great-grandmothers. All you women here are *me*. Maya Angelou.

Maria Grazia Chiuri

WOMAN OF THE YEAR 2017

When Maria Grazia Chiuri took the reins at Christian Dior in 2016—the first woman to lead the brand's creative in its 70-year history—she had a clear vision: to marry the luxury brand's legacy with a more modern, inclusive point of view. Dior had long been defined by the "New Look," the narrow-waisted, full-skirted silhouette that envisioned women as dainty, delicate flowers. "Everyone told me Dior was a feminine brand," Chiuri said. Okay, she thought, but women are more than that.

"We have to work in a way that makes it possible to dress everybody," she explained in her 2017 *Glamour* Woman of the Year profile. "I want to create collections that are wearable by different women—with different cultures, bodies, and nationalities—but still with the Dior aesthetic."

She put that in action with her first collection, in September 2016, which featured several feminist references, including a famed T-shirt bearing the title of writer Chimamanda Ngozi Adichie's essay *We Should All Be Feminists*.

The design was enthusiastically received. Adichie herself has since sat front-row at several Dior shows, and within the year Forbes was ranking Christian Dior as the most valuable apparel company in the world. In the following years Chiuri continued to infuse her voice into her designs. "You must always be courageous," she said. "Don't let others define who you are."

"Before, nobody used the word *feminist* because they thought it was a bad word," Maria Grazia Chiuri said. "The word means equal opportunity. You can be both feminist and feminine."

Alicia Keys

WOMAN OF THE YEAR 2004

By the time she was 21 years old, Alicia Keys was already a five-time Grammy winner thanks to her seminal debut album, *Songs in A Minor*. The lead single alone, "Fallin'," sold more than 16 million copies worldwide. But when Keys accepted her *Glamour* Woman of the Year Award two years later, in 2004, just after the release of her book of poetry *Tears for Water*, she knew she was only just getting started. "I have so much more to experience and say," she said. "I feel like all the greatest artists' work began when they were 30 and above."

She was right, of course. Keys continued to reach new heights in her career and activism after her award. Since 2004 Keys has claimed even more Grammys (she has 15 total), written several chart-topping albums, led just about every Most Influential list in the industry, and cofounded Keep a Child Alive, a nonprofit organization that provides support to families with HIV and AIDS in Africa and India.

She credited the women in her life—her mother and grandmother—for showing her how to be strong. "They've taught me how to be selfless and still take that mandatory time for yourself," she said. "They taught me that you can still be beautiful even with all of our flaws. And they taught me that we can walk through the fires that burn us and really try to break us and survive and be stronger for it." Though the advice was meant for Keys, it's something we can all take away.

Myrlie Evers-Williams

WOMAN OF THE YEAR 1995

In the early hours of June 12, 1963, Myrlie Evers-Williams watched in horror as her husband, civil rights leader Medgar Evers, was killed by a white supremacist in the driveway of their Jackson, Mississippi, home. It was a devastating loss: As the Mississippi field officer for the National Association for the Advancement of Colored People (NAACP), Evers had been a crucial voice in the fight for voting rights and desegregation. A crowd of more than 3,000 mourners, including Martin Luther King Jr., came to the funeral to honor him.

Evers-Williams, who had worked tirelessly alongside her husband organizing voter registration drives and demonstrations while raising their three children, was determined to see justice served. But after two all-white juries failed to reach a verdict, the prosecutors were ready to give up. Evers-Williams kept pushing them—for three decades—until finally, in 1994, the suspect was convicted of murder and sentenced to life in prison.

She didn't rest there, either: A year later Evers-Williams was elected the chairwoman of the NAACP. She vowed to restore the organization, which was going through a period of economic trouble and infighting, and she succeeded. Under her leadership the NAACP eliminated its debt and launched a massive campaign to register one million new Black voters before the 1996 presidential election. "Ultimately, it is up to us to clear the path," she told *Glamour,* which honored her as a Woman of the Year for her efforts, "to [build] an America where we make the fullest use of the great gifts God gave us."

After she left her post in 1998, she continued her mission to clear a path for the Black community—and in 2013 she delivered the invocation prayer at President Barack Obama's second inauguration. (She was the first woman ever to do so.) Her words rang clear: "One hundred and fifty years after the Emancipation Proclamation and 50 years after the March on Washington, we celebrate the spirit of our ancestors, which has allowed us to move from a nation of unborn hopes and a history of disenfranchised votes to today's expression of a more perfect union."

Myrlie Evers-Williams was a key figure in bringing voters to the polls in the 1996 presidential election. "Ultimately, it is up to us to clear the path," she told *Glamour* the year before.

"I comment only on my own experiences, and if someone feels inspired or repulsed or validated or encouraged, that's great," Alanis Morissette told *Glamour* in 2002. "That inspires *me*."

Alanis Morissette

WOMAN OF THE YEAR 2002

The power of Alanis Morissette's music is in her ability to provoke a strong emotional response through her candid, poignant lyrics. "Well, life has a funny way of sneaking up on you when you think everything's okay and everything's going right," she sings on "Ironic," the multiplatinum hit single off her groundbreaking 1995 album, *Jagged Little Pill*.

When Morissette writes, she doesn't plan to speak to millions of people around the world—but she's grateful whenever she does make that connection. "I comment only on my own experiences, and if someone feels inspired or repulsed or validated or encouraged, that's great," she said. "That inspires *me*."

When *Glamour* honored her in 2002, Morissette had just released her fifth album, *Under Rug Swept*. It was the first she had written and produced entirely on her own, a significant milestone for the famously independent singer. It went platinum within a month. In the decades following, the enduring nature of her powerful lyrics remains—so much so that an entire Broadway musical, *Jagged Little Pill,* was created in 2019 to celebrate her work.

But if it were up to Morissette, any accolades she earned would be shared among *all* women. It's why she has been so open about her own experiences with postpartum depression and anxiety. "I think any woman who's alive deserves an award like this," she said in her Woman of the Year speech. "I am grateful to be alive, grateful to be, and whatever doing this comes from that beingness, whatever form that takes, is exciting—even if that, in fact, at times does very much include sitting on the couch doing nothing. So I just want to encourage women to feel that they're beautiful and powerful, even if they're sitting on the couch as well."

Samantha Bee

WOMAN OF THE YEAR 2017

When Samantha Bee launched her talk show *Full Frontal* in 2016, the former *Daily Show* correspondent was the lone woman host in a sea of Jimmys and Johns and Jameses—a stat she didn't exactly relish. ("If I thought about it too much, I would die from the crushing pressure of it," she told *Glamour* at the time.)

But as soon as she took the stage, it became clear just how desperately late-night television needed her. Bee's blend of scathing political takedowns and groundbreaking segments, including one on the backlog of rape kits nationwide, provided a feminist voice that was very much missing, and viewers responded. More than 2 million tuned into the premiere, and ratings only grew from there. A year later, when she hosted *Not the White House Correspondents' Dinner*, the special had higher numbers than the actual White House Correspondents' Dinner telecast. It won an Emmy too.

"Sam has the rare ability to make you laugh at the same time she's stoking your outrage," Senator Elizabeth Warren told *Glamour* in 2017. "She's more than a comedian—she's an instigator and an advocate. Sam doesn't just point out injustice; she gets people fired up. Every time I watch her show, I want to stand up and cheer."

That talent for advocating was on display when Bee accepted her Woman of the Year Award. "It's wonderful to recognize women, and of course it's wonderful to be recognized," she told the crowd. "But I really do have to say that I look forward to a time when…women's equality will just be a given."

We just have too much to do, she explained. "There are so many things that need our attention, and we need to be in every room and a part of every conversation. And if we don't like the conversations we're in, we need to make other conversations that are better."

Her solution? "Let's make sure girls everywhere enter the workforce in an era where we support women, we defend women, and we believe women every single day."

"I've spent decades trying to impress people, and I just don't want to do it anymore," Samantha Bee said in 2017. "I no longer care about being rejected."

253

"THE SECRET IS, NOBODY KNOWS WHAT THEY'RE DOING."

Samantha Bee knows a thing or two about power. Every week on her TBS talk show Full Frontal, *the comedian and political commentator skewers world leaders with her razor-sharp take on their actions over the previous seven days. One memorable example: After a wave of legislative bills were passed at the state level in 2019 to reduce women's access to reproductive health, Bee "re-educated" the senators with a hilarious sex education video. As* Glamour *put it in 2017, "[Bee] delivers sermons so packed with fury and facts they often require repeat viewings." So who better to tell us what really makes someone successful? Take it away, Bee.*

THE DEFINITION OF SUCCESS DIFFERS FOR EVERYONE.

"It's hard for many people to feel truly successful in their field, because at every level of any industry there's a desire to do more."

SO DON'T COMPARE ACHIEVEMENTS.

"Even though I have my own show, I still suffer from impostor syndrome all the time. But the secret is, *nobody* knows what they're doing. I recall reading an interview with Gayle King and thinking, If she has days when she feels like she's winging it, then I'm doing okay. There are always going to be peaks and valleys in your career. How you claw your way out of that valley makes all the difference."

IT'S NORMAL NOT TO LOVE EVERY ASPECT OF YOUR JOB.

"I love having a platform to talk about things I feel passionately about, but there's stuff around my work I don't love that's a really big part of my job, like ratings and ad sales. It's all essential to the making of television but isn't something I am instinctively good at. I make peace with it because that's what it takes to keep the machine moving."

DON'T REGRET YOUR FAILURES.

"Obviously, I would love to succeed at every aspect of my job, but I try to get better every time I have another setback. A functional, equitable, and good workplace is not always the most fun to work at. It can be a painful experience to have people tell you what their feelings are, but a good manager will take criticism."

IF YOU'VE MADE A MISTAKE, LISTEN TO CRITICISM.

"You have to lead when it's really hard; 2020 has been very instructive for me in the sense that my whole staff is experiencing tremendous anxiety. There is COVID-19 and tons of social unrest. I don't know what's going to happen, so I have to be vulnerable. I'd much rather run and hide than talk about that every week in a big Zoom meeting, but you really can't."

BUT REALLY, DO NOT COMPARE YOURSELF TO OTHER PEOPLE.

"I wish when I was younger, I hadn't cared as much about what people thought of me. Now that I'm 50, I look back and go, Oh, *no one* was thinking about me. I could have been having much more fun! Everyone was all up in their own baggage."

MY CHILDREN GIVE ME HOPE.

"We're raising generations who actually care about health care, police brutality, universal basic income, and climate change and think about it every day. Would I have considered all this at 14? No, but they do, and they're going to make the world better."

Cher

WOMAN OF THE YEAR 2010

Born Cherilyn Sarkisian, Cher's dreams started early. At four years old, she said, she went to see *Cinderella* and just *knew*: This was her destiny. "I was going to sing and dance and be an actress in an animated film—because I had no idea that *Cinderella* was something I couldn't be in," she said.

Luckily for us, she didn't settle for a fairy tale. She went on to achieve greatness in almost all corners of entertainment. Her '70s series with ex-husband Sonny Bono, *The Sonny & Cher Comedy Hour,* was so popular that more than 30 million viewers tuned in each week. Her chart-topping songs "Gypsys, Tramps & Thieves" and "If I Could Turn Back Time" are so iconic she's been dubbed the Goddess of Pop. She won the 1988 Best Actress Oscar for her role in *Moonstruck. Glamour* honored her with a lifetime achievement award in 2010 for these career highs, among many, many more. "You just have a desire to do something, and I never believed in no," she said during her acceptance speech.

But Cher said it was how she handled the lows that was important. "I've had huge losses," she said. "I've had great successes. I've been so lucky. But the thing about huge losses: It just makes you keep going. I feel like a bumper car because if I hit a block wall, I just go in another direction." What she wants for everyone, especially women, to know is that they should never listen to "no" when it comes to their career, because "*no* is just some bullshit word that someone made up."

"You just have a desire to do something, and I never believed in no," Cher said in her 2010 WOTY acceptance speech.

Margaret Atwood

WOMAN OF THE YEAR 2019

In 2017, as harsh measures were imposed in numerous U.S. states against women's reproductive rights (including the 19 states that banned abortion at or after 20 weeks), women flooded state capitol buildings across the country to protest. They wore red capes, white bonnets, and somber faces. They stood powerfully in silence but carried banners and placards with their message: Our bodies, our choice.

These activists had come dressed as "Handmaids" to echo Margaret Atwood's prescient novel *The Handmaid's Tale*. Though the book was first published in 1985, Atwood's depiction of a totalitarian government that strips women of their rights has remained a constant—and terrifying—reminder of the threats women face when it comes to control over their bodies. And when it was finally adapted into an Emmy-winning series for Hulu, a whole new generation of fans were introduced to Atwood's writing—and to using the now widely recognized symbol of a Handmaid's uniform to protest rulings seeking to remove women's freedoms.

For Atwood, inspiring action is the whole point of writing—it's why, she said, she would never consider a memoir or autobiography. "I'm more interested in the story and the reader because if you're just writing for yourself, why publish?" she explained in her *Glamour* 2019 Woman of the Year profile, in which she was honored with a lifetime achievement award. "If you're writing for the reader, you're actually interested in what you might evoke for the reader."

But any young women seeking advice from Atwood might be surprised to hear her insist they don't need it. "You hardly need my words of encouragement, young women, because you are creating your own words and encouraging one another," she said in her speech. She cited women like Greta Thunberg, also a 2019 WOTY winner, as an example of how young women continue to inspire her. "Because of you, we oldies have hope for the real world. So go for it."

From her earliest days as a writer, Margaret Atwood has refused to stick to any one genre. "There aren't any rules that say you can't," she explained to *Glamour*. "There's other people— and sometimes it's you—who make up those rules, but are they really rules?"

Chanel Miller

WOMAN OF THE YEAR 2016

In 2015 the world only knew Chanel Miller by her pseudonym, Emily Doe—and yet she had changed the conversation about sexual assault forever.

In January of that year, Miller had been brutally sexually assaulted on the Stanford University campus. She was found unconscious by two graduate students, who apprehended her attacker and held him down until police arrived. "From the beginning, I was told I was a best-case scenario," she wrote in an essay for *Glamour*, under her pseudonym, nine months later. "I had forensic evidence, sober unbiased witnesses, a slurred voice mail, police at the scene. I had everything, and I was still told it was not a slam dunk. I thought, If this is what having it good looks like, what other hells are survivors living?"

After her assault Miller wanted to remain anonymous for, as she called it, "self-preservation," but she couldn't stay silent. So she wrote a victim impact statement to be read to her attacker, Brock Turner, at his sentencing that spring. He was found guilty of three felonies but was sentenced to only six months in jail—to global outrage. But her powerful words had a much greater outcome. Her statement went viral—it was viewed 18 million times on BuzzFeed within a few days of being published and was even read out on the floor of Congress. California closed a loophole that allowed lighter sentences in cases where the victim is unconscious or severely intoxicated. Her goal had been to show that she was strong, that she was a survivor, not a victim, and the world responded with a flood of support.

Glamour honored Miller as a Woman of the Year in 2016, but because she was still known only as Emily Doe, Gabourey Sidibe, Freida Pinto, and Lena Dunham were asked to read her statement on stage, to a standing ovation. Nobody knew it at the time, but Miller was in the room watching it all. "They gave me a voice when I was still not ready to speak publicly," she said later.

Three years on, Miller was ready to share her story—and identity—with her memoir *Know My Name*. "Every survivor who came before me has taught me how to be ready," she said. "They have cleared a path. I have taken my time restoring, learning how to dig my tunnel. Now I proudly walk up and join them." At the 2019 Women of the Year ceremony, *Glamour* honored her again. The moving poem she wrote to read at the event brought the packed audience in Lincoln Center to tears. Her words, in full, are included on the next page.

From the beginning, I was told I was a best case scenario.

I had forensic evidence, sober unbiased witnesses, a slurred voice mail, police at the scene. I had everything, and I was still told it was not a slam dunk. I thought, if this is what having it good looks like, what other hells are survivors living? I'm barely getting through this but I am being told I'm the lucky one, some sort of VIP. It was like being checked into a hotel room for a year with stained sheets, rancid water, and a bucket with an attendant saying, *No this is great! Most rooms don't even have a bucket.*

After the trial I was relieved thinking the hardest part was over, and all that was left was the sentencing. I was excited to finally be given a chance to read my statement and declare, I am here. I am not that floppy thing you found behind the garbage, speaking melted words. I am here, I can stand upright, I can speak clearly, I've been listening and am painfully aware of all the hurt you've been trying to justify.

I yelled half of my statement. So when it was quickly announced that he'd be receiving six months, I was struck silent. Immediately I felt embarrassed for trying, for being led to believe I had any influence. The violation of my body and my being added up to a few months out of his summer. The judge would release him back to his life, back to the 40 people who had written him letters from Ohio. I began to panic; I thought, this can't be the best case scenario. If this case was meant to set the bar, the bar had been set on the floor.

The morning after the sentencing, my phone screen was stacked with texts and I turned it over saying, not today, on this day I deserve to sleep. My phone kept ringing and I learned that BuzzFeed was waiting for my permission to publish my court state-

ment in full. As soon as it was posted, I remember thinking, what have I done, making myself exposed and vulnerable again. I texted my sister when it hit 20,000 views, thinking that was it, the comments were actually quite nice, and I closed my computer.

I started getting e-mails forwarded to me from Botswana to Ireland to India. I received watercolor paintings of lighthouses and bicycle earrings. A woman who plucked a picture of her young daughter from the inside of her cubicle wrote, *This is who you're saving.*

When I received an e-mail that Joe Biden had written me a letter I was sitting in my pajamas eating some cantaloupe. *You are a warrior.* I looked around my room, who is he talking to. *You have a steel spine,* I touched my spine. I printed his letter out and ran around the house flapping it in the air.

There was, of course, the wee sprinkle of trolls. Some photos of me leaked and someone said, "She's not pretty enough to have been raped." In response I say, damn I wish the world could see me. I wish you could see my big, beautiful head and huge eyes. Perhaps now you are at home imagining me looking like some sort of bloated owl. That's all right.

When Ashleigh Banfield read my letter on the news I sat stunned watching her speak my words, imagining them being spoken on every television set in the nation. Watching women and men at Gracie Mansion, on the floor of the U.S. House of Representatives, girls in their rooms, gathered together to read each segment, holding my words in their voices. My body seemed too small to hold what I felt.

In the very beginning of it all in 2015, one comment managed to lodge harmfully inside me: *Sad. I hope my daughter never ends up like her.* I

absorbed that statement. Ends up. As if we end somewhere, as if what was done to me marked the completion of my story. Instead of being a role model to be looked up to, I was a sad example to learn from, a story that caused you to shield your daughter's eyes and shake your heads with pity. But when my letter was published, no one turned away. No one said I'd rather not look, it's too much, or too sad. Everyone pushed through the hard parts, saw me fully to the end, and embraced every feeling.

If you think the answer is that women need to be more sober, more civil, more upright, that girls must be better at exercising fear, must wear more layers with eyes open wider, we will go nowhere. When Judge Aaron Persky mutes the word justice, when Brock Turner serves one month for every felony, we go nowhere. When we all make it a priority to avoid harming or violating another human being, and when we hold accountable those who do, when the campaign to recall this judge declares that survivors deserve better, then we are going somewhere.

So now to the one who said, *I hope my daughter never ends up like her,* I am learning to say, I hope you end up like me, meaning, I hope you end up like me strong. I hope you end up like me proud of who I'm becoming. I hope you don't "end up," I hope you keep going. And I hope you grow up knowing that the world will no longer stand for this. Victims are not victims, not some fragile, sorrowful aftermath. Victims are survivors, and survivors are going to be doing a hell of a lot more than surviving. ⊚

"Emily Doe" has chosen to remain anonymous.

Pictured at left is the original essay Chanel Miller wrote for *Glamour* in 2016.

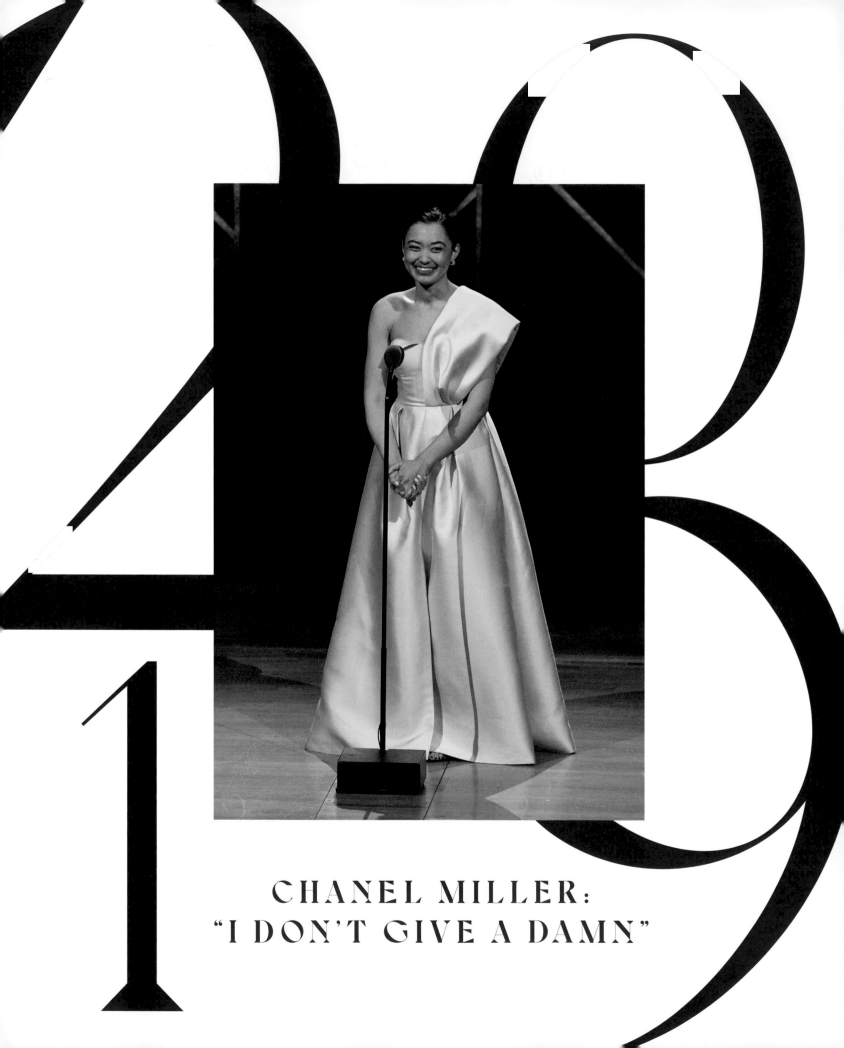

CHANEL MILLER:
"I DON'T GIVE A DAMN"

I don't give a damn what you were wearing.
I don't give a damn how much you drank.
I don't give a damn if you danced with him earlier in the evening,
if you texted him first, or were the one to go back to his place.
People may continue to come up with
reasons why it happened, but the truth is
I don't give a damn.

But I do give a damn how you're doing.
I give a damn about you being okay.
I give a damn if you're being blamed for the hurt you were handed,
if you're being made to believe you're deserving of pain.
The only reason I am standing here is
because people gave a damn about my well-being,
even when I did not.
They reminded me that I carry light
and I deserve to be loved even when I forgot.
They gave a damn.
That's why I am who I am today.

So here's the takeaway when we step up for survivors,
when we stop sealing them off in shame,
when we quit interrogating them with stupid questions.
Look what happens.
Books are written, laws are changed,
and we remember we were born to create,
to not only survive but look hot and celebrate.

So tonight you must come away knowing that I will always, always
give a damn about you the way you gave a damn about me.

ACKNOWLEDGMENTS

A special thank-you to *all* three decades of *Glamour*'s Women of the Year, whose extraordinary leadership, activism, and talent inspired this book. Because of you the world is a better place.

To Anna Moeslein, whose passion for this book is evident on every page. This testament to 30 years of exceptional women would not exist without you—and the months of research you conducted, hundreds of pages of notes, hours of fresh interviews, and many days and nights writing. A true labor of love.

Natasha Pearlman for her thoughtful edits and tireless dedication to this project. You were the first to believe in this book and understand its incredible potential.

Samantha Barry for her inspiring leadership and enthusiastic support, which was a constant motivation. Cindi Leive and Bonnie Fuller for their contributions to *Glamour* past and present. To Philip Whitney, thank you for sharing your mother's incredible work.

Sarah Olin for her beautiful design vision, and Nathalie Kirsheh for her guidance. Because of you, the pages of this book show all the women in their full power. For every powerful woman we feature, we needed an equally powerful photo, for which we thank Kathryne Hall, Tim Herzog, and Robyn Lange.

This book would truly not be possible without the careful planning and direction of Ivan Shaw, Eilish Morley, Jason Roe, Jim Gomez, John Banta, Robin Aigner, Lori Cervone, Madeline Scheier, and David Agrell. A deep gratitude to Alison Ward Frank and Caitlin Brody for their constant support, to Frank Pulice for his command of the Women of the Year archives, and Ruhama Wolle for her valuable assistance.

To Rebecca Kaplan, thank you for sharing our passion for celebrating women, and our ambition, and for wanting to create this beautiful legacy alongside us. To Shawn Dahl, Annalea Manalili, Sarah Masterson Hally, Anet Sirna-Bruder, and the rest of the Abrams team, thank you for all your work getting the book off to print during this extraordinary time.

A special thank-you to Anna Wintour for her encouragement, without which this book would not have been possible. Raúl Martinez, whose design insights can be seen on every page.

Many thanks to Christiane Mack, Christine DiPresso, Mark Lemerise, Amanda Meigher, Tamara Kobin, Angelina Rivera, Christopher Donnellan, and Kim Fasting-Berg for their support.

A deep gratitude to the former *Glamour* contributors and writers who wrote the original profiles of the Women of the Year. They are Dahlia Lithwick, Leslie Bennetts, Alex Morris, Eliza Griswold, Jennifer Siebel Newsom, Tiffany Blackstone, Collier Meyerson, Carvell Wallace, Lisa Cohen Lee, Jamia Wilson, Yamiche Alcindor, Shaun Dreisbach, Macaela MacKenzie, Denene Millner, Leslie Robarge, Sarah Wildman, Liz Brody, Sheila Weller, Laurie Sandell, Christine Spines, Louise Gannon, Farai Chideya, Marisa Cohen, Robin Givhan, Courtney E. Martin, Kati Marton, Marcy Lovitch, Lynn Harris, Gillian Jacobs, Sarah J. Robbins, Susan Dominus, Amanda Robb, Geraldine Sealey, Alison Prato, Alexandra Marshall, Kaitlyn Greenidge, Sharon Cotliar, Jessica Pressler, Elaine Welteroth, Lola Ogunnaike, Oliver Jones, Megan Angelo, Nadja Spiegelman, Julie Stone, Mattie Kahn, Melissa Harris-Perry, Valerie Jarrett, Rachel Neubeck, and all those whose contributions may have gone unacknowledged by a byline.

A deep gratitude also to all the photographers (a full list of whom you will find on the following pages), and their teams, who brought so much power and grace to the images they captured of our Women of the Year. Thank you also to all the teams who represent our Women of the Year, and who worked with us to honor them.

To all the people over the past three decades who have worked tirelessly to put together the annual Women of the Year Awards—the magic thread running through the book—a truly heartfelt thank-you. The endless dedication of all those at *Glamour,* the Condé Nast talent group, the creative group, the PR team, our long-term partners Overland, and KCD, has enabled this wonderful celebration of womanhood. To Wendy Shanker, whose words have indelibly shaped WOTY. And of course to Alexander Liberman, who designed the Women of the Year Award that remains as beautiful today as it did in 1990.

To the generations ahead—we thank you for all that is to come.

Thank You.

PHOTO CREDITS

PHOTO CREDITS
